THE TREE-WAKE[illegible]

"Oh bother!" Br[illegible] early, Alex. H[illegible] of Kew w[illegible] throu[illegible]

"Com[illegible] [illegible]e miserab[illegible] [illegible] except come bac[illegible]

As they tur[illegible] [illegible] a hand on their shoulders.

They jumped.

The arms were covered with yellow feathers. The hands were Maborian hands. The Maborian was standing behind them and he had a great shock of yellow-brown hair.

"Who are you?" they both asked.

The Maborian smiled. "They call me Kovor, you know," he said.

Keith Claire

The Tree-Wakers

Illustrated by Claire Andrews

CAROUSEL EDITOR: ANNE WOOD

TRANSWORLD PUBLISHERS LTD
A National General Company

THE TREE-WAKERS

A CAROUSEL BOOK 0 552 52016 0

Originally published in Great Britain
by Methuen & Co. Ltd.

PRINTING HISTORY
Methuen edition published 1970
Carousel edition published 1972

Carousel Books are published by Transworld Publishers Ltd.,
Cavendish House, 57–59 Uxbridge Road, Ealing, London W.5.
Made and printed in Great Britain by
Hazell Watson & Viney Ltd., Aylesbury, Bucks

To Margery Olive Latham
who has the green fingers

CHAPTER ONE

People said: "Oh, they're just the Maborians." People were really quite offhand.

Alex always asked very seriously, but the answer had always been the same.

"Those Maborians, Alex, are just a legend and a story. Yes, I know you can see them, but that's neither here nor there. Being a legend they cannot possibly be true."

Brid, his twin sister, even received a warning:

"The Maborians—you must always look away. It's better to look away, Brid. No—don't ask them any questions, whatever else you do. They are just not there. You must look in another direction."

Brid just replied with her stubborn nothing. Alex said: "Fiddlesticks"—when they were by themselves.

The twins had only recently come to stay for a holiday in Kew with Uncle Frederick. They had never seen Maborians anywhere else and they had never heard of them before. On the very first day Alex had stopped to speak to one in the street (before Brid could). The Maborian was sitting on the bonnet of somebody's car in the sun, looking into people's faces, and taking careful note of what he saw. Sometimes he laughed. He was tanned and fair and about their age. When Alex spoke to him though, he only looked back and smiled. It was a curious smile, as if he knew everything that they could remember, and could remember everything that they could look forward to.

After that they were always seeing Maborians.

"They all look the same anyway," somebody had said.

But Brid knew better. Each Maborian looked quite different.

"Much more different than us really," Alex had pointed out.

"We wear much the same things. Same sort of jeans—you borrow my shirts. Just look at them though!"

They weren't quite sure what it was the Maborians did wear, at first. Brid then decided that they must be wearing feathers, all sorts of feathers, drab feathers, dark feathers, brilliant spotted, barred and dazzling feathers.

The Maborians also painted their feet—different colours.

"Adults go about with their eyes shut," Alex remarked. "They don't see anything."

"But you are not supposed to look," the grown-ups said.

"Quick," Brid whispered to her brother, "look into this shop window."

The shop sold antiques, bric-à-brac—all sorts—all kinds of things. Usually the twins found it fascinating just to look in at the oil painting of a man-o'-war, the wheelback chair, the enormous fir-cone and somebody's grandmother's silver tea-pot. Usually they had a word with the antique dealer who often sat outside, drinking his tea from a King George V mug. Today they just looked at the surface of the glass, at the reflection of the Maborians. Squinting right into the middle of a large chest of drawers, they could see them quite clearly. They seemed to be arranging a creeper round a lamp post. They were doing it with enormous care, the twins could not quite see why. One was a girl with russet hair over her bare shoulders.

But it was as they looked that it struck them both —though Alex said it first: "You know, Brid— they're not really our age. They're old, desperately old, I think."

The one thing their father *had* told them about, before they came down to stay in Kew, was the gardens—Kew Gardens; or, as Uncle Frederick always insisted on calling them: THE ROYAL BOTANIC GARDENS.

Uncle Frederick had wasted no time in taking them round and had been full of the fact that it was over three hundred years old, that it was the most famous botanical gardens in the world, a scientific research laboratory for plants. It was the most wonderful collection in the country.

"But it's Kew Gardens," Alex had insisted afterwards to Brid, as if that explained just what he meant.

It did to Brid.

Their Royal Gardens were different to any other park they had ever been to. It was a tempting place, with a lake full of strange birds where it would be exciting to swim out and explore the four islands in the middle. There was a Chinese Pagoda, tall and red and unexpected, all among the trees, which you could not enter and yet they would have liked to have gone inside. There was even a Japanese gateway that unbelievably led nowhere.

But dear old Uncle Frederick did not seem to be interested in all that. It was botany that fascinated him. He even had his own conservatory at the back of his house—a sort of greenhouse up the wall where he grew his odd and complicated potted plants, whose names they could never remember. Though he did keep a tank there for his tropical fishes, rather a good tank with a thing that bubbled up air in one corner and a light that glowed through underwater plants. They liked watching fishes. Uncle had suggested that they might like to grow plants in pots too, but they preferred the aquarium. Things lived and moved in that bright underwater jungle. The old pots were too small and too dull—and just too slow. You didn't have *time* to wait for anything to happen in them.

But Kew Gardens—the Kew Gardens they saw—that was different. There was a twisted path that led down into a hidden valley where you could run through a maze of blossoms. Or there was the great Pond where a fountain threw water high into the air and over which two stone Kylins glared.

("Kylins, what are Kylins?" Brid had asked. She had had to ask twice.

"Oh—they're Chinese lion-dogs—I think," Uncle Frederick had said at last.)

Or there were the greenhouses (very much larger than their conservatory) where you were suddenly hot and sticky and under twisting, impossible creepers, where feathering palm fronds clutched down to reach you. There was a sense of wetness and the air was sharp and sweet with forbidden scents.

Brid liked to feel a place all round her. She liked visiting it in her way, which usually meant going there without other people and with Alex. They had been to the Gardens several times now but never actually on their own. Why shouldn't they go to the Royal Botanic Gardens by themselves first thing tomorrow morning? It didn't cost much to get in.

Directly after breakfast, they walked together down to the high brick wall with the great iron gates, topped by the Royal Arms, the Lion and the Unicorn, and the turnstile just inside, and beyond that the whole green garden waiting.

But although they had their money ready, there was no one to let them in.

"Oh bother!" Brid exclaimed. "We're too early, Alex. How maddening!" Nothing made Brid crosser than having to wait for things. The Gardens were so close. Together they looked through the high iron gates. There were the lawns and woodlands, so empty and so inviting.

"Come on," Alex said after a while, a little miserably, "there's nothing we can do except come back later."

Brid rather suspected that he was almost as miserable at her getting cross as at not being able to get in. She tried to smile.

As they turned away they felt a hand on their shoulders.

They jumped.

The arms were covered with yellow feathers.

The hands were Maborian hands. The Maborian was standing behind them and he had a great shock of yellow-brown hair.

Alex twisted, but he could not move from the Maborian grip. There was a pause and then Brid and Alex both opened their mouths at once.

"Who are you?" they both asked.

The Maborian smiled.

"They call me Kovor, you know," he said, and he said it very softly, almost as if he was trying to remember his own name. Then he looked at them, first at Brid and then at Alex.

"I know they call you Alex and Brid and Hello and Good Morning! Let me tell you that things are not always what they seem. Oh no! Certainly not at the beginning and even less so afterwards. Let me tell you that I know just those things that you think I could not possibly know and that I can see just those things that you think I could not possibly see. But say nothing, not to me, not yet, but just follow me if you dare. Gates will not stop me. I am Kovor and I am not stopped by anything. No."

He was turning back to the entrance and they found themselves following him.

"Your times make no difference to me," he said cheerfully, producing a large and extraordinary key from under his feathers. "This fits most things you know."

With half a twist of his key the lock slid over and the gates swung open.

"Can we really come in now?" Alex asked shyly.

"You will have to come in now," Kovor replied gently. "For in fact it is we who have summoned you, we who they say are a story, who they say do not exist, and who must not be spoken to. When we call, those whom we have called must come. And that is not all, no, for you have been summoned by the Molk himself, summoned to stand before HIM —and when HE summons, even Kovor, that is me, must answer."

He seemed to smile to himself, and he was all in his feathers of yellow and he was waiting.

Brid and Alex did not dream of arguing. They just went with him.

The Gardens were wonderfully green.

CHAPTER TWO

Kovor did not lead them along mere paths. Rather he turned half left, away from the Palm House and its pond with the fountain, away from other people, away from paths, straight and free over the grass.

"It is quick we must be, otherwise we shall be slow and be late and even in trouble, and that would not do, and isn't this beautiful?"

"Where are we going, Kovor?" Brid asked.

"That is a good question and it will be answered by going there."

Kovor was striding forward now at a tremendous pace—it was a job to keep up with him. They went under the trees and through the copses and even picked their way over the flower beds. Brid was sure that this must break somebody's rules, but it was impossible to argue with Kovor, he was going too fast.

Away to their left was the enormous flagpole on the mound. Uncle Frederick had told them that it was two hundred and twenty-five feet high and had come from a single fir tree. But somehow Brid and Alex had never seen a flag on it. It had always stood there high and bare.

"Look," Brid said impulsively—Alex was already looking.

Today there was a huge green banner streaming in the wind and in the centre they could just make out a red and golden flower.

"Who's the flag for?" Alex wondered out loud.

"That is always flown when the Molk himself is in High Council which he is today, you see, which is why we are hurrying because we are at it."

"But who is the Molk?" Brid asked.

Kovor looked intently from Brid to Alex and from Alex to Brid.

"When we arrive at where we are going we shall indeed meet him and how else do you know who somebody is except by seeing him yourself?"

That's true, Brid thought. That was the sort of trueness that she agreed with and felt safe about.

But then, Alex decided to himself, as he ran a bit to keep up with Kovor, you had to see people lots of times really to understand them and then it was useful to hear what other people thought about people, even if it only told you something about the person who was telling you.

All at once they were coming up to a high square glass building, very large and white and set on a green bank above them, with a flight of tall steps leading up to a pair of enormous doors. Over the entrance there were the stone figures of a King and Queen. Brid and Alex had never been in here before. Kovor led them up the steps, two at a time.

On one of the doors, in large letters, there was a notice saying CLOSED.

Kovor led them at full tilt towards it when at the last possible moment it opened—and Kovor stopped.

Another Maborian stood in the doorway, taller than Kovor (good-looking, Brid thought,) with a precise face and eyes that seemed almost closed. He had one hand just slightly raised to halt Kovor's onrush. They all stopped on the threshold with a sudden jerk.

"Oh—here we are. Now this is Corbrey, you know, and I had better tell you that he's our Master of the Candletrees and Minister of Protocol and don't ask him what protocol is or we shall all be here until tomorrow and later for certain if we arrive at all. Hello to you, Corb."

It was Corbrey's feathers that impressed Alex. They were completely and sleekly black, each one perfectly in place. Corbrey's long face did not move a muscle at Kovor's greeting, the eyelids were hardly raised. He spoke in a huge, hushed, and reverent whisper.

"The High Council has *begun*. The Molk himself is seated."

"Oh, we are late then. I knew that we would be. Why did you not use the sense that is in your head, Corb? Did I not tell you, you nutskull, to hold back the proceedings for an extra five minutes by using your brains? A practice cup of coffee before the first cup nobody would have refused."

Corbrey appeared to ignore the interruption completely. The Minister of Protocol addressed himself entirely to Alex and Brid.

"Welcome to the most splendid, the most high, the most glorious Council of Great Maboria in Exile," he whispered to them. "When you get inside it will be a *great* moment, a great moment. In the far distance, in the far, far distance you will see on his throne, the Molk. You must of course *bow* at once. Then you must go forward *ten* paces and then you must *bow* again."

"And mind how big those paces are, you two," Kovor put in, "because if they are too big it will be bowing into his lap that you will be doing."

Corbrey's eyelids opened completely. Brid could actually see that he had large brown eyes.

"Kovor!" Corbrey's reproving whisper was a kind of gasp. "Now, Alex, and you Madam Brid please, are you ready? We will all go in."

Brid found her hand being taken firmly by Kovor. They all went in.

They had come into a different world. Here it was warm. Suddenly they had stepped into a huge forest under glass, a strange forest full of palms with tall, round trunks reaching upward and upward and topped with green fronds that arched high above their heads. Here and there, between the huge drooping fan-like leaves, there were splashes of bright flowers and thick curtains of tumbling green creeper. Alex could hear the sound of water bubbling—and the scent, the sharp, exciting tropical smell of strange plants came thick to his nose.

But from the doorway, from their feet, there was a long red carpeting of camellia petals that led to the foot of the very tallest palm of all.

"The Honey Palm itself, that it is," whispered Kovor.

"The *Jubea Chilensis*," Corbrey murmured.

On either side of the rich red path—all at once the twins saw them—there were Maborians, Maborians standing shoulder to shoulder, or sitting or squatting, dark skinned or fair, boy and girl, boy and girl, all in their different coloured feathers, silent and waiting, smiling and watching. Suddenly Brid realized that this was, to the Maborians, a most important occasion and an occasion when they possessed all the time in the world.

Kovor and Brid and Alex and Corbrey all bowed. Brid and Alex were amazed at themselves for doing it, but they could not help it. Ahead, all their eyes could take in were golden banners hanging from the tree trunks, and then they went forward over the scarlet carpet; and as they did so, a single trumpet from high above them rang out a silver fanfare of clear cold notes in the silence that echoed and re-echoed from the great glass roof above the treetops, and then they all four bowed again. Alex saw all the faces of all those Maborians on either side of him and then they were going forward a second time. Then he really saw, seated at the foot of the Palm Tree, seated and silent and motionless—they both saw—the Molk himself.

The Molk did not look at them directly, he stared forward and over them, he stared above their heads.

"Good morning," he said.

It was a very deep voice, Alex noted. The Molk was very big, much bigger than the other Maborians about them. His feathers were larger and in sombre reds and gold. His feet rested tremendously on the ground. Why, Alex thought, he's got golden toenails too; but there was nothing girlish about the Molk. He could have picked up Kovor even, and held him over his head with only one hand.

They found themselves looking up and up at the Molk, up and up at the Honey Palm behind him, the *Jubea Chilensis*. They were just aware that he sat on a very plain tall chair before them and that he was flanked by two other, two very different Maborians on either side.

"Good morning, Sir," Alex and Brid just remembered to say.

"If," the Molk began.

There was a very long pause. Slowly and thoughtfully the Molk was scratching at his left ear.

They waited. Everybody waited.

Brid had to stop herself from bursting into a giggle.

"If—" the Molk's tongue explored right round his lips as if he were searching for the last of breakfast. "If you have quite finished *bowing*, Corb," he said very heavily, "you might see your way to clear a little space, some room round about, and then perhaps we can get on with the Council."

He alarmed Alex by now addressing him directly: "A chap likes space in which to think. That's my opinion. Can't think when there are a lot of other people all jostling around, cluttering and fidgeting."

Corbrey bowed again, all by himself.

"Yes Sir, of course Sir, at once Sir," he whispered and then he turned and although neither Alex nor Brid took their eyes off the Molk, they heard a lot more whispering and they felt, rather than heard, the many Maborians behind them move, slide, just drift away under the palms.

"That's better," the Molk remarked with obvious satisfaction. "Now you are Brid and you are Alex. Don't be surprised that I know. I know most people —when I remember—always have a tremendous amount to remember."

Now they were shaking a huge hand, Kovor was finding them stools and they were seated before the Molk and before a very long low table on which stood a high grey jug and a long row of grey bowls. And suddenly it all seemed to Alex to be a perfectly

natural place for Brid and himself to be. It was as though they had been here every day.

"Now before I begin," the Molk said slowly.

Out of the corner of her eye Brid could see him scratch his other ear. She looked away.

"I suppose everybody ought to be introduced so that you know just who is and who isn't. Well, you both know Kovor. He's the one that's sitting over there—just got himself a bowl. Er—you both know Corbrey. He's the Master of the Candletrees and Minister of Protocol and whatnot, wherever he's got to. No, don't bother to bow again, Corb, we are being quite informal."

Corbrey only whispered but both Brid and Alex heard every word.

"We are not *supposed* to be informal, Sir," and then he sat down opposite them.

"And I," came a honeyed voice that was anything but a whisper, "am HARRAGONG—in case dear Moli forgets to mention me. Molkeza of all Maboria, Archmaborien, in charge of both everything and absolutely everybody and simply roaring to go."

The voice was a tornado of dark laughter travelling through the twins' ears and they found that suddenly they had eyes for nobody except this almost black Maborien. Harragong sat in a shimmering whirl of peacock feathers, with her chin on her knees. She was regarding them with a tremendous, enthusiastic amusement. The warm brown eyes not only met theirs, but chuckled right through them. Alex felt that even when she sat still, she was moving. He watched her put her feet down on the floor (silver toenails too, Brid noticed) and Alex was certain that just as the Molk was quite incredibly strong so Harragong was. . . .

"Today we can BEGIN. Today I am an infinite number of years old—which makes it my birthday—which is sheer bloom on the blossom. But don't be ALARMED. I don't expect you to send me a card. I don't even expect you to wish me a happy birthday—I've got one already. But I'll tell you your most important secret of the day—you won't even be expected to give me a present—you see you ARE my birthday present, Brid and Alex. Hello!"

"Hello," they said, a bit bewildered.

"Harri," a thick, guttural, difficult voice was speaking right into their heads. "Must you prattle ven our guests are avaiting their refreshment? Coffee? Ja—before my fellow councillor exhausts you vith all her amusing celebrations. Alvays I brew the coffee vith mine own hands, for no vun makes it the vay I do."

He had been sitting on the table itself. His hair was white, not silver but white like a white rabbit, and it was going wildly in all directions. His green eyes were simply swivelling over them out of his beaming frog-like face.

"Kovor, vill you pass our guests the coffee vich I haf brewed vith such tender care. Alvays I look after the stomach and then the stomach vill look after you. Drink! I recommend. Feel it go down. Enjoy! Vonderful!"

His face came to within inches of their own.

"I am the Ludaz. At these High Councils I am vot they call the Think Man. Ven they haf a problem they talk about it. Ludaz thinks about it. Then I say vot I think. Then, out of my vast experience, they know vot to do. Also I vatch over the Maborian stomach. I brew the coffee. No vun knows the secret. If I could die, that vould be terrible. But I cannot die. I go on. I brew."

His feathers were a shining green—he was hugely pleased with himself. Brid and Alex found bowls being pushed into their hands by Kovor.

It would be coffee, Alex thought dubiously. But there was Brid drinking hers and she usually made such a fuss. He sipped. Well it wasn't too bad. In fact—mmmmmm—this was different.

"Jolly good coffee," Brid declared.

It was jolly good coffee! Corbrey was whispering to Harragong. Harragong was talking loudly to Corbrey. Everyone was pushing bowls to everybody else.

"Order, order," the Molk demanded. His coffee had been drunk.

As the Molk he got it first. Ponderously he put down his very large and ample bowl, double breakfast size.

"Umph! I think that you have all said enough. Now I am going to do the talking. The rest of you can sit, drink, and listen."

The big hand pushed the big bowl down the table in the direction of the Ludaz and the third refill.

The Molk sat back in his tall chair, his feathers rustling. He seemed to be remembering what he was about to say.

"We knew you would come," he began.

There was a silence. He looked at them inquiringly.

"You mean us?" Brid asked.

"I mean you," the Molk said. "Both of you."

Alex looked up at the huge frame in the chair.

"We didn't know we were coming, Sir. We just came. We don't know what we've come to. You see—nobody would ever tell us—who and what you really are."

"No," the Molk agreed. "Nobody would. They wouldn't want you to know. They don't want to know themselves. Well, I'll tell you. We are the Maborians. We come from Maboria, which has always been. In all times and at all places has it existed. And we, we too have always been since the beginning of the beginning. Since memory began have I been Molk of all Maboria." (Corbrey stood up and bowed) "and has Harragong been my Molkeza."

"And Archmaborien," Harragong reminded them.

"Archmaborien and dear Molkeza," the Molk agreed. "I can also tell you that Maboria is not *in* any particular place in your world. Indeed, just as Maboria has always been, so it exists everywhere. But to see it, to cross over to it, that requires a bridge, a door, a way through. Though it is always very near, it is, at the same time, always very far away."

Brid looked from one to other of the feathered Maborians, sitting about the table, with a new curiosity.

"What's your Maboria like?" she asked.

The Molk's face stared into the distance and then he smiled.

"Ah Brid! How can I tell you? How can I help you to understand our country, our city and our home? Maboria—one is never tired of Maboria. But to describe it. . . ."

He paused for a long time and then, quite obviously, he decided.

"No. I won't try to describe it. I'll begin by showing. To see and to smell and to hear—that is to know."

He stood up.

For an instant Alex wondered what was going to happen. The members of the High Council were all on their feet—he was on his feet with Brid beside him. The Molk looked taller than ever standing in his red and golden feathers, more splendid, more frightening perhaps and strangely somehow sad.

Then Brid gave a little gasp, for from behind the tall chair Corbrey appeared, staggering under the weight of a huge double-bladed silver axe with a black shaft and a scarlet tassel on the end. The Molk took it from him easily, taking it in one hand, and then, beckoning to the twins, he strode away down the Temperate House, everybody following closely on his heels.

At the far end there was a pair of doors. Brid and Alex followed the Molk through. They had come into a strange glass room with eight sides. It contained only a tree.

If it was a tree. . . ?

It simply stood. It was high and white and gaunt, white as a candle reaching to the roof; but it was like a stake, for it grew no branches outwards, there were no leaves upon the end.

The Molk halted at its foot. The trunk of the naked tree was thick, yet the Molk had only to swing back his axe the once—he seemed to Alex to look at his tree without seeing. And then the silver axe whistled into the wood and through the wood with an enormous force. The Candletree gave a fearful groan. For an instant it stood still, as if resting on a pedestal, and then it tottered—falling slowly with a tremendous certain dignity, falling as the Molk required, at a first and single blow.

Alex and Brid found themselves being jostled and pushed by Maborians—not just the Council members, Alex noticed, but all the Maborians. They had reappeared in their countless feathers, they were crowding eagerly around, elbowing their way forward.

"BACK," the Molk roared. "Back upon the dread and awful penalty of my extreme displeasure. For the Candletree is cut. I have not cut it at Yesterday. Today is not the time to look at Yesterday. I have not cut it at Tomorrow. Today it is not our business to gaze at that which is to come. I have not cut the tree for you. I have not cut it for your beloved Molkeza. I have not cut it even for my dear friend Thobrusk. The tree is cut at Today, not for the Maborians, but for their guests."

Corbrey had taken back the axe. The Molk had turned. He did not glance at the fallen Candletree himself. Alex and Brid found that he stood before them. He bowed. He took their hands.

The Molk was smiling. A look of great pride spread slowly over his face. He said very gently:

"We grew the Candletree that you might come and see Maboria. Madam Brid, and you Alex, come with me, for I want you to see for YOURSELVES."

CHAPTER THREE

The sharp axe of Maboria had cut both clean and true. The twins looked at the fallen trunk, at where it had been cut, at the rings of growth that were a fantastic design. Here now . . . forcing itself upon their attention through the hot, sticky, growing smell of the greenhouse, was a different scent, an aroma coming from the white and fallen tree, an essence of morning-sharp air, a tang of woodsmoke. And as they looked within, the pattern of the tree was clear, like a map of time, like a view out of a dark cavern and into a world that seemed to grow on for ever. And now they could hear the sounds of water bubbling, water splashing on to tumbled stones. They saw the gleam of polished rock and rich brown shadows in furrowed bark, sunlight on leaves, and roots reaching down. Here too the wood-smoke, blue and hazy, wafting and lazing its way towards . . . and in that distance tall spires grew and pointed up to catch the sun.

Kovor's voice was almost singing in their ears. "There you have our city, the climbing towers of Maberdy. In Maboria our houses grow and ripen in the summer sun, brighten and change colours down to russet reds. Our houses are alive and so to live in one is also to play an instrument, to know a friend and sing a song. See, blue water flows through spaces like a honeycomb, in streets, along avenues, meadows surrounded by mansions, great birds strutting over bridgeways, longboats gliding down corridors of silver water, rivers rising up transparent columns, streams tinkling down stairways. Our people, plants and places live at many levels."

But the twins did not only see, they were there. They smelt and heard and their fingers might have stretched out to touch. They were being drawn into the calling distance of the tree, they were Brid and Alex standing in the midst of Maberdy. Yet where were they, and where were Harragong and Ludaz, and although the Molk's hands were on their shoulders, where was he?

"Come here," came Ludaz's voice from a long way away. "Come, Bridder. Ven the Candletree is cut, then must vun only gaze."

"When the Candletree is cut," Alex heard the Molkeza say, "then you are today, but already today has become yesterday."

Brid found that the Ludaz had drawn her back.

Alex could only see the Molkeza now—she was smiling, yet looking anxiously into his face.

"I'm better now," Brid heard herself say.

"Look outside, look out both of you," Harragong told them firmly, and they were turned towards the windows. "Breathe three times and tell me what you had for dinner yesterday—go on, tell me."

"Shepherd's Pie," Alex said vaguely, shaking his head rather like a dog trying to get a fly out of its ear. Somehow he could hardly see.

"You'll do!"

Alex just stood there, not seeing through the window, seeing only the many feathered Maborians standing about him, and still the birds and houses of that far Maboria.

"They will both do," the Molk pronounced slowly. "I think they have done very well."

Alex seems to be all right, Brid thought, but she wasn't at all sure that she was. She seemed to be thinking with only half her mind. Maboria was still with her.

"So—so that is what Maboria is like," was all she managed to stammer out at last.

"E-X-P-L-O-S-I-O-N!" Harragong declared.

"What's that, my dear?" the Molk inquired.

"Explosion! That's what Maboria's like too." Harragong leaned forward and grasped Alex by the wrists. She looked right down into his face again. To Alex it felt as if she was looking right into his head.

"Have you ever known the privilege, have you ever gazed upon the fearful flower of Olbaboth?"

Alex was dazed. What was she talking about?

"No, Ma'am."

"Ah—that is a day for life when the Winehorn

sounds aloud. Then will you see at last our mighty flower. That Olbaboth is found tallest on the inmost Lake of Grey and Green of far Maboria. You must wade into the shallow lake. You climb the tree. You gaze into the flower and with your eyebrows you feel —you listen with your fingers and know in Olbaboth the pulse and centre of all Maboria beat."

Harragong let go, her words still ringing in Alex's head. Now her attention stabbed at Brid.

"You could hunt with Harri. Gallop, ride astride a hound, Brid, and net the Ignet Seed—the erupting zestful parachute. Sound your horns and you capture it, struggle with it, take it home and feed it. Make it your own. Teach it to sing. When people come to hear—don't just play on your house like an instrument. Stand still and let it play you. That's what I call conversation with friends—you talking, other people listening. Explosion!"

"That too can be Maboria," the Molk agreed.

"But not only that Sir," Corbrey whispered fiercely down the table. "Maboria is the place where you are *free*. Nobody in Maboria ever asks you what you are growing or when it is going to seed, and no one either comes or calls unless you want them to."

"You listen when I call," Harragong pointed out.

"Only if I want to, Ma'am, and of course I always want to."

"Und also," the Ludaz pronounced, "I can tell you, Alex und Brid, that all this growing, all this playing, all these expeditions und plantings need a great deal of thinking about. Even Corbrey's house has to be cultivated. If you feed your house vith the wrong thing it vill fall down."

He nodded knowingly in their direction.

"He who plants the Olbaboth must know vat he is doing. Othervise—even ven you are immortal—you haf the discomforts."

"But here," the Molk said gravely, looking slowly round the octagonal glass room and out at the tidy lawns beyond the windows, "here we are finding it hard to grow the Olbaboth. We are in a land that is not Maboria. Here we are strangers. Here we are so far from home."

He sighed. "So far from home," he repeated almost to himself.

Brid was upset to see that the big face had become enormously unhappy. The huge Molk looked suddenly so fragile.

"We have only hope," he continued, "hope, that one day we can return again."

"But," said Alex incredulously, "you mean Sir, you *can't* go home. You can't get back to Maboria?"

The Molk shook his head. It was Kovor who answered.

"No, Alex, we cannot go home. Not yet. Here we are stranded. Here we must stay. We found the way here you see—oh many years ago—we found a way through, a bridge over and a gate in. A wonderful adventure it was, a chance to explore this world that is yours. But also we made another discovery, that the gate we had closed behind us would only work in one direction. Nothing we could do would open it again. Trapped we were, and are too, even now and today. Unless we find a new way back, we cannot go home."

For Alex, the bridgeways of Maboria, the strutting birds swung irresistibly before his mind. But Brid was beginning to imagine what she would feel like if she had to stay at Uncle Fred's for always; if she could never again count all those chimney pots from her own bedroom window, or walk with their father through their own dusty square with the high and grey, grim but familiar church that sat there in the centre of it all.

For a long time no one spoke and then Corbrey said softly:

"Sometimes, when I was at home, I would pole my longboat down the corridors of Maberdy. Perhaps I would visit Vorsche—he who is so silent—who carves the scents and fragrances. . . . He does it in his twining workshop underneath the waterfall. His work speaks for him and I would talk to it for hours. But how long is it since I saw him build a perfume at his bench? Or there was Trota with his cities full of bees. He would take me in to bow to Queens, taste honeys—one's tongue more deafened by the sweetness than the ear by hum." Sadly Corbrey shook his head. "This does not happen here."

"Kew is a very beautiful place," Kovor put in, "but it is not so beautiful as Maboria. In Maboria there grows the Great Harp, higher than a tree, higher than a hall, and there I would play. But I could not bring the Great Harp with me when I came to Kew, another would not grow, and so now Kovor can no longer play and has forgotten how."

"You see," explained the Ludaz, "in your land so many things are made, so few are *grown*, und ve find this most strange. Ve came as a most scientific expedition to discover your vorld. Ve made a great exploration und it vos so enjoyable und then ve made our greatest discovery. Ve had lost ourselves. But still—ve haf the good hope. Here, gathered together in your Gardens of Kew, ve haf the most formidable collection of Maborians that haf ever left our great country. That vos vy I, the Ludaz, vos chosen as the Think Man. That vos vy the Molk und Molkeza came in their persons. That is how, cut off, exiled und lost, ve haf still here, in these strange houses that ve haf found, been able to entice a shadow of Maboria to grow. Ve haf not despaired, for here at least ve can still verk, research und struggle—here ve can try too to grow a new vay home."

"But do you think you will ever be able to do it?" Brid asked with concern.

"Well," the Molk replied slowly. "No—and yes. That is—I mean, well we are getting somewhere perhaps. . . ." He scratched an ear. "There *is* a way. That is why you are at this meeting. That is why—well. . . . You see, we invited you. . . ."

"You are our guests," Kovor broke in.

"It is a great honour," Corbrey breathed.

The Ludaz smiled hugely from one twin to the other.

"I can tell you, vether you like it or vether you do not—you are the very next item on the agenda."

"This," Harragong said with a great rush, "is why you are my birthday present."

"You see," the Molk began again, "we Maborians cannot manage it on our own. But if you . . . if you were to help."

"Of course," broke in the Ludaz, "there is no *earthly* reason vy you should . . . ve just thought."

"If only you would," implored Corbrey.

"And I'm so looking forward to it," declared Harragong.

Brid and Alex looked at each other. They smiled. Twins, they did not need to speak. Alex knew but Brid answered. Without hesitation and for both of them she said:

"Of course we'll help."

CHAPTER FOUR

Suddenly all was noise.

A ringing fanfare of trumpets echoed round the tall palms and trees, the brilliant blossoms, the feathery leaves and creepers of the Temperate House. The assembled Maborians (there seemed to be more and more of them, Brid thought) were cheering and waving. The Molk himself was shaking the twins by the hand. Alex was alarmed to find the Molkeza taking him by the wrist and dancing him round in a ring.

"Well it was that I knew you would volunteer," Kovor was saying.

"It is a great honour to thank you," Corbrey whispered.

"Ah!" the Ludaz exclaimed. "Our good friend Thobrusk said you would be sure to agree. He is alvays right."

Brid and Alex felt slightly uncomfortable.

Then the Molk lifted up a hand for silence. He was so tall that he needed neither throne nor platform. There was immediate quiet. Everybody paid attention. He smiled at the twins and at Harragong. He looked gravely round the assembled Maborians. The dark red and gold of his feathers gleamed as he spoke.

"This is a good moment. Certain difficulties are before us. If we fail, we know that it may be hundreds of years before a way back to Maboria could be re-opened. It would be a longish wait."

He paused.

(He's going to scratch his ear, Brid thought. There—he's scratched it.)

"If it fails—it will be the fault of us Maborians. Our guests, Alex and Madam Brid, will do their best. We ask no more. If they fail it will be because I—and you—will have failed to show them how. What they will have to do will be hard. We alone know how hard it will be. Whatever happens in this great experiment, they will need our help—and whatever the result, they will receive our thanks."

Everybody clapped. There were cheers.

Brid and Alex began to feel a little better.

"NOW . . ." came a powerful thrilling voice through all the noise. "NOW at last we can do something."

It was the dark and black-browed Harragong, Molkeza of all Maboria, who spoke. At once you could have heard a seed drop. With a great sweep of her feathers she turned towards the twins. Yet in spite of all her overwhelming majesty her voice was friendly, her glance was understanding, even though she sounded grave.

"I must tell you, Alex and Brid, that to help us will not be easy. And we can only help you so far. We can only try to prepare you for what is to come."

There was a great approving murmur all round.

"What is to come?" asked Alex seriously. "What will we have to do?"

Harragong shook her head.

"That you can only find out from all of us, slowly and bit by bit. For to open the way back to Maboria you will have to understand our Maboria, get to know our Maboria, recognize Maboria. You will have to follow a programme that will show you the powers that we have, the instruments that we use, the very sap by which we live. Only then will you be able to know our final secret, and have the knowledge to ripen our escape. We cannot open up the way ourselves; we can only open your eyes, so that you may see what is there when at last the time comes. You will have to trust us. You will have to begin our programme with one of us. Begin with my great friend and adviser, the Minister of Protocol: Corbrey, Master of the Candletrees."

Another cheer went up to the roof.

Corbrey was bowing to his toes.

"Oh Madam—it is an honour indeed."

He actually spoke out loud.

The twins hardly knew where they were. They found Corbrey leading them through a little door at the back and suddenly they were alone with him and it was quiet.

Once through the door, everything was unexpected. You went down two steps and into a different place. They were still in the Temperate House but here the building was low and built of dark wood. There was a different warmth and it was pleasant here with sandy paths and earth under the feet.

Corbrey paused. A little shy, he waited for them. His black feathers were still sleek and perfectly brushed.

"This is my little place," he said modestly.

It was comfortable. He had bookcases round the walls filled with many-coloured volumes. There were three carved and curving chairs crouching together under a bush of camellias in front of a rusty rug, waiting for someone to sit. There was a table, polished and long, shining and black, where you could look at your face. There were implements on the table, implements for the garden, silver and of many sizes, with handles carved with faces. There were hoes and trowels, forks and tiny shears. They were clean and perfect and waiting to be used.

Brid wanted to touch.

But there were the roof-beams. This was what caught Alex's eye. They were strung with great lanterns. There might have been twenty of them there, hanging like burning baskets, spiral and bulbous or conical, or like great red eggs luminous upon their sides. They were made of bright threads, masses of inter-twining multi-coloured threads that twisted up and round, crossed over and re-rose to form a rainbow pattern. They were lanterns that glowed like old embers or stared with shining green.

Alex was taking a closer look.

"They've each got something inside," he declared.

Corbrey allowed himself a tiny smile.

"These are the first things that I shall show you." He reached up and lovingly caressed one of the lanterns in his hands. In spite of its glowing appearance it was cool and ancient, and nearly rubbed away with care. Slowly he spun it round on the end of its chain, so that they could see. Tiny lights seemed to wink and change all about their heads and to be reflected in the glass walls all about.

"How beautifully they're made," Brid said wonderingly, hoping that Corbrey would let her take one down to hold.

"These are my cages of pure time," Corbrey whispered. "Inside each one I keep a piece of time, Maborian time, as you keep tea inside a vacuum flask. Inside its cage each piece of time stands still."

"Is that what I can see inside?" Alex asked. He was on tiptoe now. He wished he could stand on one of the chairs.

Corbrey shook his head.

"Time is hard to see. It is not time that you can see in there. But do not try to see yet, Alex. Listen! Listen Brid! What do you hear?"

And then he held the lantern still and they listened, they listened hard.

It was like a wind.

"The wind of time," Corbrey whispered. "Only a little wind because it is only a little time—but always it blows. Maboria is not only a place, it is also a TIME, a time in which to live, an age in which to endure. To travel from where we are to where Maboria lies is not only a journey—you also have to slide into another time. Just as you might slide your hand into one of these time cages."

"Can I put my hand inside?" Brid asked eagerly.

"But what *is* it I can see in there?" Alex still wanted to know.

Corbrey laughed, a little soft pattering laugh, and he slid his hand inside the glowing lantern. Then quickly he withdrew it again and he was holding . . .

"Why," Alex exclaimed, "it's a tiny Candletree."

"If we snapped it—could we see Maboria again?" Brid asked.

Corbrey looked from one to the other and nodded solemnly.

"When a Candletree is alive it grows through time. It is a living record of the whole history of Maboria. If you cut it exactly in the middle, you will see the present. If you cut it lower down you will see Maboria's past. If you cut it above, you will behold its future. When first you cut the tree the record is alive. Soon it becomes still, like a photograph, and then powders away. What you saw today is Maboria as it is now. All Candletrees carry this our history and because it is the same history, every Candletree shows the same thing if you cut it in the same place. Even this little sprout here. But the bigger you let the tree grow, of course, the bigger the picture will be and the more accurately you can cut it. However a Candletree takes a very long time to grow to any size, so you do not cut them often. Many hundreds of years must first go by. Only when you want to ask a very important question of either the past or future or when you want to remind yourself about today."

"But why should people want to know what is happening today?" Brid asked.

"Many people live only in the past, or spend all their time dreaming of the future. Sometimes it is more necessary to know the present, as you needed to know on joining us today. And then for us it is even more difficult. You see Maboria is an immortal land—Maboria never dies. I too am immortal and I shall always be."

"But surely—" (it struck Alex all at once) "the time will come when your history reaches the top of the tree. What will happen then?"

Corbrey looked at the Candletree, small and

white and helpless in his hand. Gently he bent it round so that the bud of the tree was twisted back into the roots. He held it there with thumb and forefinger for a whole minute and then took his finger away and showed them. The Candletree had grown into a ring.

"Time takes long to turn," he said "Each circle takes ten thousand years. When we come again we will have forgotten almost all that we have done. Maboria never began. It has always been. The circle revolves. The record remains locked tight within the living Candletrees. Only one of us, the Molk himself, can remember all the way and even he must keep his memory green each year by opening up the trees."

"But if you look in the Candletrees and see what is going to happen," Brid suggested, "and if the Molk can remember, then you will know if you are going to get back to Maboria."

Corbrey was carefully easing his little Candletree back into its time cage. The light within seemed to flicker for an instant. Again they could hear the blowing of the little wind.

"Oh yes, that is quite right. We know that we do go back *eventually*—else the circle would not join and we should not be here. But we do not know exactly *how* and *when*. You see the Candletrees grow only through Maborian time and will only yield the history of Maboria, it will only tell us what is happening there. Not here. Again, our Molk remembers all the journey round, but his mind is burdened with so many memories. He does not bring up *all* things clear for fear of disturbing all the memories below. He can only tell in which direction our way home may lie. He can only tell that what will happen will be due to you."

"But what," asked Brid, "will you want us to do?"

Corbrey looked back from his swaying lantern. He looked round his room with the books and the growing camellias and his waiting chairs. And then he closed his eyes completely and his voice grew quieter than ever.

"The first thing that you will have to do is just to reach into our time—to reach out into circling Maboria. You must plant your own, your most particular and splendid Candletree. You must touch our time. See here." Corbrey opened his eyes abruptly and quickly led them over to another cage, a hanging lantern on the other side, a lantern burning gentle blue. He lowered it on its chain.

"In this cage," he explained excitedly and his fingers slid all round its surface as he showed it to them, "a new Candletree can be planted. They can only begin in Maborian time. This is where you are going to plant your Candletree. This is where you are going to take a part in Maborian time."

For a moment Corbrey fumbled in his feathers, deep in his black feathers, and then at last brought out a small, exquisite speckled pouch. Looking very solemn he opened up its throat.

"Here we have a single seed. From this seed you will be able to grow your Candletree. You will then possess a true piece of Maboria that is your own."

It was a tiny delicate silver pod. With great care Corbrey deposited it into Brid's hand. The twins exclaimed because it shone. Corbrey closed Alex's hand over his sister Brid's. They had to kneel down together, hand to hand. They had to thrust their closed hands through the rainbow threads, into the cage, into the earth, into Maborian time.

Corbrey stood over them.

For a single instant the twins felt themselves held together, held in a great rush of well-being that was flung through them. They thrust together, into the earth.

Brid saw a bright white flash.

Alex heard an intense ripping sound.

Corbrey gave a piercing scream and snatched them backwards.

Like a molten fist a blazing white-hot double tree rose out of the bottom of the cage, rose upward like a rocket, burst the threads, burst the cage, burst the glass above it, towering and twice above the Temperate House itself, sliding upward, growing fruit, giving shade, spreading . . . and like a bubble vanished into nothing.

Brid could smell an essence of morning-sharp air, a tang of woodsmoke.

"The last seed," Corbrey wailed. "What has happened? The cage? Our time? What has happened to your tree?"

There were tears running down his face. The twins were still groping, blinded by the light. The chair was knocked over. Alex was brushing glass from his sweater. The camellias were bent.

"What's happened?" Brid asked wonderingly, a little stunned.

"It is all right. It is all right," came the thick and comforting voice of the Ludaz from just behind them. "Corbrey! Corbrey! Vot did I say? This proves my idea, my theory, vot I expected. Madam Brid und Alex, you are all right? You may not know it, but it seems you are more strong, more powerful than our time, our Candletrees. You ver given a Tree to plant—but you haf sent it back full grown to our Maboria instead. Mark my vords, Corbrey. Ve shall not be far behind."

CHAPTER FIVE

The twins were uncertain as to where they were. They knew only that they were outside, in Kew Gardens, and hurrying under high trees. The Ludaz strode along between them, a notebook held open in his long fingers. He just went on making calculations:

$$\text{OA} = \sqrt{x^2 + y^2 + z^2 - (ct)^2}$$

He wrote without looking as he walked.

Corbrey was dazed, scurrying along with them.

"What does he mean?" Brid asked Corbrey, still half stunned herself, but not so stunned as to have lost her curiosity.

"I never know what he means," Corbrey gasped.

Alex was still recovering from the explosion. He had been impressed by the other Maborians. It was only too obvious that they had been as shocked and surprised as Brid and himself when they rushed in. Perhaps almost more so. But how they had moved. Shattered glass had been whisked away. The Candlecage, or at least the twisted remains of it, had been approached with particular care, the pieces picked up with long and delicate transparent tongs, untouched by even Maborian hands. Ludaz had taken charge, for Corbrey had been quite dazed. Maboriens had calmed the shaken plants.

"But what have we done?" Alex asked. He still wasn't really sure.

"Done—" Ludaz said, snapping his notebook shut. "You haf done a miracle. My scientific mind is alvays surprised by a miracle, but then the scientific mind is being given surprises every day. Life can be very exciting—yes? Bridder, how do you like making the new discoveries—no?"

Brid was not sure that she did.

"No," the Ludaz agreed. "There is one thing better than making discoveries und that is comprehending them. Perhaps ve vil all do this after not too long. You haf returned a Candletree to Maboria—now perhaps ve vill all return. In the meanvile ve must all continue with the Molkeza's programme."

Brid was beginning to recognize where they were. They were coming up towards the Lake.

There was nobody about. The sun shone brightly and the Gardens seemed very peaceful. Lines of trees stood waiting as far as the eye could see and there was the long water with the ducks and geese in motion, proceeding like ships to distant destinations, dipping downward sometimes, dabbling for feed, sending bow waves from their blunted feather prows. A moorhen, treading carefully through the undergrowth gave its honking, haunting cry.

The twins had always liked the Lake. But now there was something here that they had not seen before. A solemn Maborien was poling expertly in a curious and fragile boat like an immense leaf that floated almost above the surface of the water.

Ludaz caught the prow with a green and skilful

foot. The Maborien crouched in the stern with her pole, beckoned them aboard. There were no seats. They just had to crouch with her. In a moment the delicate boat was gliding from the shore towards the islands.

"Uta vil take us to the Root," Ludaz explained from the bow, indicating their pilot. "Uta is almost more of an authority on the Root than I am. Uta vil take us to the island. On the island is the Root—und Uta."

"I always wanted to know what was on the island," Brid began, with a sidelong look at Uta. This Maborien was very different from Harragong. Uta had a thick plait of auburn hair and her feathers were as green as Ludaz's own. Brid still wasn't certain—did the Maborians wear their feathers, or did they grow them? Whichever way, Uta's feathers were incredibly trim and there was an expression in her eye, an absolute look of attention. Brid found her almost alarming.

Alex had to admire the way Uta propelled her craft, it was too shallow to be a canoe, with such complete confidence and skill. He could not see how she managed to make them go so fast. Neither did she look back at him as Harragong had done, as if to overwhelm him, take him over, make him do something. Uta was simply interested in him sitting there—in the same way as Alex found himself to be curious about her.

"You cannot see the island properly from the shore," Ludaz was saying. "It is the central island ve are heading for."

"Why are we going to the Root?" Alex asked.

"Vy do ve go to the Root? Because it vil be most

important to you. But vot it does und how you may verk it, ah!—that you vil find out ven you make the arrival."

There was a jerk. The boat had circled right round the islands to the other side and at this moment it pulled up sharp. Alex had never felt anything like this in a boat before. Uta had stopped them like putting the brakes on hard in a car. They all fell forward. She reversed them up towards the shore.

"Come," Uta said. She had a voice that knew exactly what it was doing. "Let us go and look."

She skipped out of the boat, held it with her foot and put out a hand for Alex who would have to disembark first. Small though she was, her grip was like steel.

Alex entered first. He could feel the others coming behind him. *Entered* was the word. He had not thought that an island could be like this. It was like a room without a roof. He could still hear the remarks of the passing duck, the faint plash of water. But here one could not see the water. He was in a circular space with trees, with trunks, with roots rising, tight close to each other and all surrounding, and only the blue sky up above their heads. It was like being at the bottom of a well. You could not see the edge of the island; only round roots and trunks going upward.

"You are at the centre of the Root," the Ludaz announced.

Brid looked up at the twisted knotted wood, at the roots writhing and twining. There were no leaves, there was only bark branching, fingers of wood moving outward and dividing above them.

And then Alex looked at the back of the "room". There were ledges going up in stairs with keys—piano keys going round in tiers of semicircles as far as the hands could reach. Between the steps there were rows of long buttons, each button end carved—with a distinct and individual face.

"It must be—it must be an organ," Brid exclaimed. "Are you going to play? What do you play on it?"

But there was a shocked gasp from Corbrey.

"Nobody plays—you do not *play* the Root."

The Ludaz only smiled, his eyebrows rising at their ends.

"The Root, my dear Bridder, *you* do not play the Root of Maberdy. Let me tell you—the Root plays *you*. Vatch—vatch closely my dear Alex und Brid, my friends—for Uta vil show you vot happens—oh it is an experience."

Alex stared fascinated over the shoulder of the little Maborien, who settled herself on the seat before the Root and tucked back the auburn thick plait over her shoulder.

"Now," she ordered. "You will pay great attention." Her hand moved over, far over, to a button on her extreme left.

"Look at the button, at the button she presses," Ludaz murmured.

Her finger hung poised over one solitary button carved with its face. The face, small and perfect in every detail, was her own.

"For every Maborian in exile there is the button," Ludaz explained. "The Great Root at home is much bigger for there is a button for every citizen of Maboria. Here ve haf only the members of the expedition."

"And you can only play if you press your own button?" Alex suggested.

"It vil play *of* you—if und ven you press your button," Ludaz agreed.

"But what sort of sound is there when you play—when it plays . . . Uta?" Brid wanted to know.

Ludaz shook his head. It was Uta who replied.

"It does not play sounds at all," she said shortly. "I will begin and then you will know."

She pressed the button, the button with her own face and then they saw her hands go up and move over the keys—they saw the fingers splay outwards and press down. But it was as if the fingers were pulled down by the keys themselves, as if Uta was receiving the Root's message through her finger-tips.

Yet this was not quite true, Brid began to realize. She did not hear anything herself. She just knew what the Root was playing, just as she knew that she herself existed. It played in her head.

"She's in Maboria," Alex whispered, for he knew too. In spite of their own shoes they knew warm leaves under their feet, they walked across a round green place surrounded by green arches, many growing arches on all sides and rushing yellow water entered under one and hurried out another. They walked through a tall and creeper-covered opening, they knew an endless wooden room. They stepped lightly. They felt feathers against themselves. There were books upon the walls, metal books in silver, copper and gold and there were more books upon a table before a coloured window. When they turned the pages there was a strange writing that they could read in a weird language—yet they could understand. There was a pleasure in knowing, in following at speed an argument—the subject of which they had not heard before, in an unfamiliar language with someone whom they could not see—and winning.

Brid suddenly knew what it was to be both young and old. Alex felt, just for a moment, what it must be like to be a girl. He could feel a plait give a gentle tap between his shoulder blades. . . . They were Uta—and then she stopped playing.

"Oh but this is only a taste, my friends," Ludaz was saying excitedly, rubbing his hands and hopping all the time from one foot to the other. "You summon the Root most beautifully, my dear Uta. But now the Alexander und Bridder must try it for themselves."

"But what is it?" she asked. "How does it work?"

"Does it happen—does it happen like the Candletree?" Alex suggested thoughtfully. He had found the journey exciting, but there was something he could not understand. "That *was* Uta—something Uta did," he added. He gave the little Maborien a searching glance—he had not actually seen Uta while the Root had played, rather he had been Uta.

"No, Alex," the thick, heavy voice began again, "the Root is different from the tree-trunk und it is different in two ways. Firstly, it only sees back, und then, unlike the Molk, only a little way, only as far as *ve* can remember. Secondly, you can only see out of the Root through a *person*. It may be yourself, it may be somebody else, but it is limited, it is vun person's view. The Candletree's whole ring in time, that is Maboria, is a whole ten thousand years around.

But, as Corbrey should already have told you, only the Molk himself can remember that far back. For the rest of us, our Roots trail behind for perhaps seventy years. Yet that is enough. It is very real."

"Why do you need the Root though?" Brid asked. "What made you bring one with you?"

Uta sat in her place before her complicated keyboard and to her it was simple. Brid felt that for Uta their questions were simple too. For Uta everything was straightforward. But there was something in her green-eyed smile that reassured Brid. Uta did not laugh at her.

"Why yes," Uta said, "why did we bring this Root with us? So that we should always know about ourselves. So that we could always see again our own opinions and our own points of view. But even more important—the Root could show us again the points of view of our friends. We are immortals and so we have to live with each other for ever. When you are immortal you can never escape your friends. So you see it is important that we understand each other. A tune only works in your head when you know both ends of it. A person is only understood when you know both sides of him. You see the outside—you must also see and know the inside—and with the Root you can also see what he has behind him."

"That is vy," Ludaz put in, "you must know the Root to know, to discover, Maboria. For unless you know Maboria you vill not be able to open the vay back to our great country. Show them Uta. Show them the nexter thing."

"Oh yes. Brid, you must sit here, Alex, beside your sister."

The twins sat.

Brid began to work it out.

"This is Corbrey's button," she said, finding his neat, handsome features carved right on the button in front of her nose. "And here is the Molkeza's next to it. That could only be Harragong. Then there is this button with a hood over it. Why do you have the hood?"

"Because it is the important vun und ve did not vant you to look at it until the time has come. Und that is now!"

The Ludaz removed the hood with a flourish. It was a much larger button and there was not one face carved upon it—there were two.

"Us," Alex declared.

"Press," Uta said urgently.

"You must press," Corbrey whispered.

Together they pressed. Their hands were drawn upwards, were drawn over the keys. Softly, certainly, intensely, they touched.

They found at once that it was different from when they had heard? . . . seen? . . . known? Uta's playing. This was themselves.

For they were running. Without running out of breath, they were running over a giant field of scarlet poppies, a field sloping gently down. Again their feet were bare, there was the velvet softness of petals under their toes and they were running faster and faster. They were not running after anything. They were not running away. They were simply running.

Perhaps, and only perhaps, there was just a shadow in their minds of the Root Room, of the three Maborians standing behind them; but they could not turn round, they could not look about them.

They had stopped. They were stock still in the centre of the vast field of waving poppies. Before them, it was a long way away, at the very distant end of the field . . . they felt a rising edge of excitement . . . there was a wide and shining green lake spreading outwards—and springing up from the centre of its surface a fountain of transparent leaves that flung themselves forth in eightfold clusters and climbed up to the height of a tremendous tree. And at the very top a final crown of foliage surrounded a gigantic and unopened bud that shone like some most splendid cupola.

. . . And they heard a shouting, a shouting far away, like cheers, like praise: "Olbaboth. Olbaboth."

"But stamen und stigma," cried Ludaz, abruptly interrupting the playing, "they haf never been there und they haf *remembered* it! You haf not been there—tell me that you haf not been there—but I know you haf not been there. Uta! Uta! Vot has happened? It is so unscientific. They haf remembered down the Root a thing that they haf never done."

"No, we have not been there," Alex was saying softly. "But I remember it now. I shall never forget it."

"Oh dear, oh dear," Corbrey was whispering. "Everything is going wrong. Everything is happening the way it doesn't. Everything today seems to be doing what it didn't. The Candletree grew in a minute and now they are remembering what they haven't yet seen. Oh dear, oh dear."

Only Uta appeared to be unperturbed. She stood back thoughtfully, absent-mindedly sucking the end of her plait. For Uta, everything was a matter of course.

"My dear Ludaz, to me it is simplicity. Alex and Brid are remembering a piece of their past that they have not yet got to."

In the distance Brid could just hear the quack of a passing, drifting duck.

CHAPTER SIX

"Ven vun is faced with the insuperable problem, an impossible difficulty or a hopeless situation, vun STOPS. Vun has the lunch."

Perhaps, Alex thought, an insuperable problem had been expected, or possibly an impossible difficulty had been anticipated or perhaps, even, nobody was surprised when the situation was found to be hopeless. There was quite a gathering waiting for them at the Orangery, ready and prepared for an official, formal and traditional Maborian luncheon.

Alex and Brid remembered the Orangery as a rather strange white and empty place, with dull marble statues and a few green shrubs sitting about in tubs by tall and stately windows. The scene was different today.

The Maborians had made great preparation.

At the far end an elaborate carpet had been unrolled over the cold floor—a carpet of blues and gold. Brid could make out the peacocks worked into the pattern, with big dogs bounding and trees twisting. In the middle of the carpet Alex observed, with some satisfaction, an oval table laid with a delicate

net-like tablecloth and simply bristling with high glasses, with a curious shining silver and with many dark and polished wooden bowls, where the lines and whorls of the grain danced and swirled in fascinating patterns.

But dominating even the table, hanging on the long length of the plain back wall, lending a great colour to the entire Orangery, was an immense green tapestry, complicated, intricate and involved. Here, rising out of a land of cascades and meadows at many levels, they could see tall rods of Candletrees leading up from end to end to where, in splendour and unmistakable, were the woven forms of the Molkeza and the Molk upon their thrones. High above their heads, glittering over the length and breadth of the tapestry—was a glowing flower of golden red.

And waiting for Brid and Alex....

"Hello-o," Harragong called out to them as they came forward, and she was waving frantically as if she had not seen them for twenty years. The long black hair had been brushed forward over one shoulder; she was in her blaze of peacock feathers, she was brown, laughing, and Brid saw that there were now blue blossoms in her ears.

"Nothing like a good excuse to come on in and FEED. I am so glad we are having this awful emergency so that we could invite you here. Come over and sit down so that we can begin. We are all terribly and tremendously gasping. You must be absolutely STARVING."

"Come over here Madam Brid," the Molk said, beaming. "Never mind if our programme seems to be doing the unexpected. It was bound to happen. Just you come and sit by me."

Eagerly Brid and Alex moved over to the table, Kovor was pushing a chair up under Brid and Corbrey pushed one up under Alex. The twins sat side by side before the huge net tablecloth, Alex next to Harragong and Brid next to the Molk. Then the others took their places, Uta beyond the Molk and Corbrey beyond her, and on the other side Ludaz was next to Harragong and Kovor beyond him; and at the far end....

"That person down the end there," Harragong said in an undertone that made the windows rattle, "is THOBRUSK. He is very retiring and quite informal, so just pretend that you have known him all the time—he already knows everything about you—and a bit more."

"He is," the Molk said impressively, right into Brid's ear, "the Vintner of all Maberdy. There are precisely ten thousand vintages in Maboria. Thobrusk knows them all." The Molk nodded sagely as if that explained everything.

Brid looked cautiously at Thobrusk. He was a tall Maborian, almost as tall as the Molk himself and because he was thinner he looked, when sitting down, almost as if he was taller. He had a long face and very long ears and his feathers were a kind of mottled mixture of tired maroon and fusty grey. But it was the expression on that face that Brid saw. Thobrusk knew, she knew he knew, but also, as he looked at her now almost shyly, yet with enormous kindness Brid realized with a sort of shudder that he understood her, completely, to her very last thought, through and through. He appeared to be eating a piece of cake from his side-plate, and they exchanged glances, and liked one another.

But already Ludaz was talking again. He had stood up. He lifted the lid off the very largest bowl that stood in the centre of the table. A great mist rose from its centre, the air was filled with a clear fresh flavour, a kind of shining sweetness. He looked round at every one—he smiled—his eyes simply sparkled.

"Und this, my friends, is the famous traditional dish that begins all truly important Maborian meals; but today it is prepared according to a new recipe. . . ."

"From your great friend Zadul!" everybody chorused.

("It's always from his great friend Zadul," Harragong whispered confidentially to Alex. "What? No, I don't know who Zadul is. Ludaz just gets all his recipes from him.")

"From my great friend Zadul," Ludaz agreed complacently. "Do not ask me, nobody must ask me, how it is done before they haf tasted und tried. Pass up all your bowls und let me fill them to the brim with this glorious gastronomic experience."

Alex and Brid had their bowls passed up first. Alex was viewing his place at the table with some alarm. He had just realized that there was no knife and fork! He nudged Brid and they exchanged looks. They each had a small ladle, a silver hammer, a long, narrow polished tube and a gleaming pair of miniature pliers.

Brid nudged the Molk.

"What's that my dear? Don't you worry. Just

watch me and you'll soon find out. You start with the ladle."

The bowls were passed back. Alex wondered what it could be. Harragong passed him his. She winked. It was heaped to the brim.

They were . . . peas?

Not just green peas—though some of them were a smokey green—but also peas incarnadine and peas of saffron yellow—and they were so bright, it was as if they shone.

"But its the TASTE that matters," Harragong murmured loudly into his ear, bubbling with excitement. "Put that ladle down into them and lift them up to your lips."

Alex tried, tentatively. They glowed in his mouth, they seemed to shine down into his inside. He lifted the ladle to his lips a second time. This was the way to eat peas.

"Und my dear Harragong, you are alvays in such a hurry," Ludaz interjected as he continued to pour out tender-coloured peas into the warm wooden bowls. "Let our guests look. Let them feast their eyes und their noses first so that their tongues may make ready. Vun should not GOLLOP, Harragong. Otherwise it is finished with vun half of the enjoyment gone and the other half not started. Is that not so, Molk?"

The Molk, who was now consuming steadily, continued to chew with his mouth firmly full. There was a big blissful expression in his eye. He shook his head. He was obviously busy.

"It is better to eat than to talk," Uta announced. "Ludaz, I have not yet got my bowl. Thank you."

"Some of us," Harragong insisted, "can do two things at once and enjoy both of them."

Brid carefully tasted the peas for herself. The taste was sparkling—it was as if she had never eaten any food in her life before.

"The Maborpeasc are perfect," the voice of Thobrusk came sailing down the table, a voice a little weary, as if he understood too much, as if the amount he knew was almost more than he could bear, but a voice that was very clear and calm. "It is a dish that in Maboria one must always eat before one touches wine."

He nodded at Brid, expressing a kind of ancient enjoyment as he ate.

(It seemed to Alex that while the other Maborians looked young and seemed incredibly old, Thobrusk looked old and yet somehow was incredibly young.)

"We brought all our wine with us when we came," he explained. He blinked, very slowly, as if his vision was sliding down the years. "We brought many plants and seeds. We have grown them in the glasshouses and the gardens here at Kew. But our wine we could not make outside Maboria. This we already knew and so we brought great wineskins with us. Wines do not worsen when age overtakes them. They improve, they ripen, they mellow and soften, they change their character, they stay. At last and by degrees and slowly, they fade and gently turn away. Unlike ourselves they are not immortal, but their lives are long and by their flavours can we tell the passing-by of time around our circle of infinity."

Already the bowls were empty, and it was Kovor who came and collected them.

"Did you enjoy them?" he asked in his lilting voice. "But then I knew that you would, because they are wonderful, and a beginning that is now over. But do not mind, for you have all the middle before you and even the end."

"And the great thing," Harragong reminded them, "is that when you have finished you have reached that wonderful moment when you can start all over again."

She wiped her mouth on the back of a huge white feather. She looked at Alex as if to ask him, as if to invite him to read all the thoughts in her head.

"For in Maboria," she went on, "you can always do things again. For to everything we do, the circle of our time returns."

"But aren't you ever disappointed?" Alex asked. "I mean disappointed when you find the same old thing again that you've done before?"

"Don't you ever get bored, Harragong—always coming back to the same place—doing the same thing time after time?" Brid asked.

Harragong laughed. She always enjoyed herself when she laughed.

"But I always forget what I *do*," she insisted. "The time's too long. Only Moli—only the Molk out of all Maborians—really remembers all the way round."

"That's right," the Molk agreed heavily, gazing sadly at his now empty place-mat. "I remember. But then you see I don't *do* anything—very much. I just look down into my memories, at the rest of you coming and going, doing and dozing. My looking is your doing."

"At least," Brid remarked cheerfully, "you've never met *us* before." But suddenly it dawned on her. "Oh—but if you really do go round and round you *must* have met us." She looked aghast. "But we've never had lunch with you before—have we Alex?"

Harragong laughed again.

"I like you two," she said, "because you are both right and wrong and wrong and right at the same time. Aren't they Moli?"

The Molk looked extra wise.

"They are often very right," he said.

"They are often very wrong," Uta remarked.

"Sometimes," Ludaz put in, "they are a great deal cleverer than any of us."

"They are only a little inexperienced," Corbrey whispered.

"And that," Thobrusk pronounced in measured tones, "may only be another way of saying that, unlike us, they have no cobwebs in their heads."

"But we all think they are marvellous and that's pleasing to start with and even better when you remember it," Kovor urged.

"But surely—" Alex protested.

He was interrupted by the Ludaz.

"It is not the question, my dear Alexander, of *never* having had lunch vith us. From another point of view you are *alvays* having lunch vith us. Just think of that—perpetual luncheon. Ah! Is this not bliss? Only, in your case, you only experience perpetual luncheon once."

"The Ludaz means," Uta explained crisply, "that

while Maborian time is circular, your time is linear, and the two times always touch at exactly the same place only."

"Just supposing," Kovor suggested, "that you were both to come to Maboria, why when you went back we could return you to the moment you had left."

"Before we go any further," Thobrusk announced rather above their heads, for he was standing behind them, "may I explain to our guests that in Maboria we do not drink our wine with food, but only between foods." In his hands, almost in his arms, an enormous golden bottle lay. He did not let them ask any more questions. "Our traditional and formal meal has three courses for eating divided by two for drinking. Now we drink to think more deeply. Later, we shall drink to think more clearly."

Brid had never drunk wine before. She was not quite sure if she ought to start now, but then it was Maborian wine and anything Maborian, she reminded herself, was always different. Her glass (it was a very tall, pale glass on a long slender stem) was being filled with a yellow, sparkling liquid. Thobrusk seemed to shamble dustily round the table in his fusty feathers, but the wine was poured perfectly and not a drop was spilled.

It was the Molk who lifted his glass first.

"To the Return," he said gravely.

The Maborians and Brid and Alex with them lifted their glasses too.

"The Return," everybody echoed.

They drank, slowly and carefully, sip by sip.

They thought, they all thought....

It did not seem strange that when they spoke,

each Maborian talked softly only to his neighbour and that none of them spoke directly to the twins. It was as if, Alex thought, they had suddenly been left alone. For the first time he was just with his sister. He could sit here looking at the Maborians just as if they were strangers, as if they were nothing to do with him at all. They sat, in their different coloured feathers, turned away from Brid and himself. He could see the huge tapestry to one side, to the other he could look out through the tall windows across Kew Gardens. The taste of the wine, that was here; but it was a taste that you forgot as soon as you swallowed and the taste did not matter. He spoke to Brid, just quietly. Brid always understood. These Maborians might have their world, but he and Brid had one of their own.

"Do you remember our Beach, Brid?"

She nodded, remembering—the adventures last summer holiday, exploring the deserted early morning beach, looking for driftwood and curious shells and the tide coming up to cut off the bay so that it really did become their beach, their retreat where nobody else could come. They had clambered over rocks and when the tide retreated a little way they found that it had left a pool, a pale clear pool where seaweed grew and little creatures swam. And they had spent all day there, eating their picnic as the sun broke through the mist, bathing comfortably and dabbling at old dried seaweed and talking about seagulls and what it must feel like to fly.

"Remember the little crab running through the shallow water, lifting up his claws and threatening us," Brid said.

Alex remembered. They had wondered what a crab must feel like too.

Now they sat here contentedly. Looking up they saw that Thobrusk was standing between them. His hands—knobbly hands—were resting gently on their shoulders.

"When the tide finally went out," he said, "then you had to go home again—but it was worth it, wasn't it—even afterwards when they asked you where you had been?"

Alex just nodded.

Brid could not be surprised.

Thobrusk simply knew.

"We want to go there again," Brid said.

"I know," Thobrusk replied. He shuffled his feathers and looked at them and smiled an ancient, understanding smile.

CHAPTER SEVEN

"Now this, my friends," the Ludaz announced, rubbing his hands together, his eyes swivelling back and forth to be certain that he had their full attention, "is the most important moment of our most serious meal. I, the Ludaz, the think man, advise everyone to give their full concentration und then a little more consideration after that. The next dish is most rare, most unusual und it has been prepared according to a traditional recipe quoted by none other than...."

"Your great friend Zadul," everybody chorused. (Brid and Alex remembered to chorus it too.)

"That is so," Ludaz acknowledged with some surprise. "How did you know? But it is a most marvellous recipe."

But Brid was still thinking back. Alex was thinking back too.

"Alex," Brid whispered. "I wish someone—I wish just someone, just one of them, would explain what we shall have to *do* to help."

"This is going to be FUN," Harragong cried. "Here's yours, Alex."

"What you *do*, Brid," the Molk explained with a careful grin, "is this."

They were like footballs on the plate. They were big purple footballs.

"You put a tube against the side, somewhere near the top, and hammer it carefully in, so that it goes down towards the middle. Then you put your lips to the tube and suck, and mind, as you do, that you tap the fruit gently with your silver hammer."

Very gravely the Molk sucked—and tapped.

Alex, with much curiosity, took hold of his football. It felt furry—oddly furry, like a deep thick velvet. It did not wobble to his touch; it was almost as if it was growing off his plate. He picked up his tube and his hammer. Experimentally—he tapped.

Corbrey's ecstatic whisper echoed down the table. "This is quite the most *satisfactory* fruit."

"Don't be AFRAID of it," Harragong advised with a shout. "HIT TO THE HEART, Alex. GO RIGHT IN, boy."

Alex hit and his gleaming tube sank down into the flesh.

"There is no need to apply great force, little Brid," the Molk remarked. "Just know what you are going to do and do it with complete certainty and the fruit will give before you."

Brid looked up at the Molk's serious brooding face and then knew that she would try to open it just like that. She put her tube against the fur. Very gently, quite deliberately to prove the Molk's words, she gave it the very lightest tap—yet she thought right down into the fruit.

It was not the tap. The tap was only like knocking at a door. Irresistibly her tube sank, was drawn down to the heart of the fruit as if the fruit itself was calling.

The twins drank.

It was unexpected—a shock—intriguing.

There was no taste at all.

It was like drinking complete energy. Alex could feel electricity running round his ears, sheer power to his toes. Brid could feel the ends of every living hair on her head, the ends of the lashes of her eyes, even on her arms and her legs. She could feel the edges of her fingernails tingle. There was wonderful energy to run and run and yet....

... there was no hurry to spend it. It could wait. It was enough just to have, to possess and to hold.

"Ahhh!" the Ludaz pronounced. "The Globes of Generosity haf been prepared to a peak of perfection."

Harragong was literally glowing. The Molk remained seated in glorious satisfaction. Kovor sparkled down the table. Corbrey's eyes were tightly shut. Thobrusk sat alone and endlessly serene. Only Uta did not share the general joy.

She looked down her tube with one eye, her hammer clenched in her hand. Uta was cross.

"You can tell your friend Zadul that pip block is a most frustrating complaint."

She gave an expert whistling blow. She rapped the sides of her globe with her hammer, a sharp tattoo. She sucked. Uta looked up with grim satisfaction.

"Clearance has been obtained."

At this point Brid saw Thobrusk climb on to his feet again, nod towards Ludaz, and come round the table for a second time. He had a different wine, a silver liquid in a bottle in a blue-black basket. He shambled as he came, he shuffled his feet along the floor, but his glance missed not a face. He came round the table, filling as he went: Kovor, Ludaz, Harragong ("Fill it FULL, Thobrusk!"), Alex, Brid, the Molk with his deepest dusty bow, Uta—now sucking furiously, Corbrey. Before he sat again, he filled his own glass and turned towards the company.

"We drink in order that we may think—more clearly."

There was a hushed silence.

Uta looked up and said: "Not forgetting that when we think clearly, then we have another duty; we also speak more clearly, we explain."

It was Alex who saw Harragong shake her head and wink at him, saw her swig the silver contents of her glass back in a great excited gulp. Then she laughed.

Brid jumped.

"NO! We explain nothing to Brid and Alex. They have got to explain us. We are Maborians, my dear Uta. We are today, yesterday and tomorrow. We do not explain. We ARE. Let Alex and Brid find us out

—here and now—and I the Molkeza of all Maboria propose it."

Corbrey's whisper rustled down the table.

"They must wait. Time must be given a chance to tell them."

"Surely it is the hearing of the right tune—they must sing the right song," Kovor reminded them.

The Molk looked up. He had been very busy up to now.

"Patience learns best. Time and patience. Patience and time." He nodded to Corbrey.

Ludaz hammered on the table with his silver hammer.

"The Vintner. The Vintner. He is going to let us have a toast."

Thobrusk had risen. He gave a slow, an almost weary smile as if what he was seeing he had heard so often, many and many times before.

"Maborians in Exile here assembled, I Thobrusk, Grand and Undoubted Vintner, offer, as is my right most immemorial—this Toast: To our twins!"

"Our twins," everybody echoed.

(Alex and Brid remembered not to drink. Alex blushed.)

Then Thobrusk spoke again, slowly, wisely, yet with a hint of infinite amusement, his glass glittering in his hand. He spoke only to the twins.

"And now," he said, "at last the turn is yours."

Alex was not surprised at what Brid did. Perhaps it was the effect of the first wine that made him see so fully. Perhaps it was because of the second wine that Brid did speak so clearly.

She got to her feet, and began.

"But Thobrusk, none of you are telling either of

us anything—not directly. You all just keep hinting. You're like the grown-ups outside the gardens. And none of you agree. How can TIME tell us anything if we don't know any tunes, any of your tunes anyway? You say we are following a programme, but we still don't know what our part in it really is. You're always about to give us a clear answer, but nobody ever really tries to do it."

There was a flat, dead silence. The Maborians sat still, looking in front of them, all except Thobrusk, who just watched Brid and smiled—a peculiar smile—as if he knew. But Brid had not finished. She put her hands on the table now, and her feet apart, and she was just drawing breath.

"If you are immortal, that must mean that you have always been and have never started—so how can you have *birthdays*? Because if we are going to help you, then we think we ought to know. And then of course we're curious too. We'd also like to know things that don't matter. Do your feathers grow on you? Or do you put them on? And maybe you'll think these are all rude questions, but then rude questions are always the ones you most want to hear answered."

Thobrusk nodded. But Brid still hadn't finished.

"And why don't grown-ups want to see you although they know about you? And what do you *do* outside? We saw you going about the streets lots of times. Where were you going? And what did you really come here for? All we know is that you can't get back. Well?"

But Thobrusk was looking at the Molk now and then at the Molkeza. He put down his glass. He looked very pleased.

"They are wonderful, Sir—are they not?"

Brid found herself sitting down and a bit pink and everybody was clapping.

"MARVELLOUS," Harragong cried. "I have been simply BURSTING to say it all the time. Of course you want to know, Brid. And of course we don't agree. That's what makes us so interesting. We must all be different. And yes, we are going to tell you all the answers—at least Kovor is—and I can tell you now that, yes, we do grow our own feathers, *and* we can take them on and off afterwards. And of course we are like the grownups, because we are super grown-ups really, without any of the disadvantages. One question you haven't remembered to ask though—so I'll answer it in advance—what are the pliers for on this table? Well I'll show you. Taking the seeds out of toothfruits. CATCH!"

Brid and Alex only just managed to catch two small, crimson-coloured, moonshaped fruits.

"Today," Harragong declared, her black hair frothing over her shoulders, "we shall BEGIN."

CHAPTER EIGHT

"We have quite a little walk now," Kovor said afterwards, "because it is a long way that I have to take you, which is a good thing as I have a lot to tell you, which is the part of the programme that is mine; and Thobrusk is coming as well in case I forget what I have to remember."

It had been a rather rich and overpowering lunch. Alex and Brid were glad to be stretching their legs again. The early summer sunshine suddenly seemed to be particularly bright and warm, the Gardens particularly green, the trees more tall, the early leaves more lush than they had ever been before. Brid gave a little skip beside Alex. All her impatience had ebbed away—almost as if her outburst at lunch had itself done more to satisfy her frustration than any answers could have done. Indeed it no longer worried her if the Maborians did sometimes seem to talk in riddles—that was their way. And was it really riddles? Maybe—in fact probably—they meant precisely what they said. Brid gave another little skip and was pleased to see that Alex was looking happy. She felt remarkably contented now, ready to face what was coming next, or almost ready to accept nothing happening at all.

Thobrusk was loping silently alongside Alex, moving with his long stride and carrying his tall staff. There were people about here, visitors to the Gardens; a woman pushing a pram down the path ahead of them, a tanned girl sun-bathing in a blue bikini on the grass, two men in suits, intent with a camera, photographing magnolias. The baby crowed at Thobrusk as they passed the pram. Nobody else took any notice of them. Kovor even jumped over the girl on the grass, but she did not seem to see. He made faces at her. She was unaware of him.

"You see," Thobrusk explained to Alex, "they don't *dare* to admit we exist. It would upset all their ideas. According to them we *can't* exist and therefore we *don't*. But, as it happens, we *do*. They find this so unsettling that they just won't admit it. We Maborians find your adults very interesting persons, so different from ourselves. This was really one of the reasons why we came here. We wanted to inspect your peculiarities."

"What peculiarities?" Alex asked, a little indignantly.

"Anything that is different from oneself," Kovor explained, "anything that is different from what one is used to, you know, that is a peculiarity. Now let me say to you and Brid that anything that is different about you from anyone else, why those things are your peculiarities. They are the most valuable things you have got. They are what makes you and proves that you are nobody else. Where would you be without your peculiarities, I ask you? Nowhere, because you wouldn't *be* at all. For instance, not all your grown-ups cannot see us. Sometimes, not very often, I am surprised. Somebody sees me, somebody's eyes are open, somebody gives me a smile. That is worth keeping. The same way—not every child can see us, you know. The other day I met a small girl who could not see me at all. But I did not mind. I was interested. I asked myself why (I always like to ask myself why), and added this girl to my collection. I have a wonderful collection of peculiarities, you know. Almost as good as the Molk's."

They had left the path now, and were going under the trees.

"Was it to get our . . . peculiarities that you had this expedition to Kew Gardens in the first place?" Brid asked.

"That is one reason why we came here," Kovor admitted, with a grin. "We all wanted to improve our collections. Like stamps, you know."

Alex was beginning to feel rather intrigued, but an odd thought crept into his mind.

"But how did, do you collect? I mean, it's not like butterflies, is it? You don't pin people out, or shoot them like big game? I mean, you don't put their heads on the wall?"

"Why NO! By the Tree of Olbaboth itself, what a suggestion! It's not like that at all."

Kovor was shocked. Thobrusk was amused.

"No, it is not like that," the Vintner assured them, with a quiet smile. "You see, everybody has a pattern. It is rather like knitting, only much worse. What it is all made out of even has a name: deoxyribonucleic acid, though I don't often pronounce it. Well, when we see a peculiarity, a particular pattern, we write it down and then—here is the exciting part—it is *grown* into a Maborian plant for our gardens at home. So each plant is unique, complete with its own peculiarities. The Molk has the biggest collection and the Ludaz the most unusual. Uta, of course, has the most complicated."

Thobrusk permitted himself another smile and then thought for a moment.

"Kovor's collection is a very good one. People say that Kovor's is the most beautiful."

Brid saw Kovor look away.

"But you can't grow people into plants," Alex said doubtfully.

"No, not people you can't," it was Kovor who corrected him. "Not people, but the patterns of people; that is different as you will discover. You will not be able to escape making this discovery, for the Molk will never let you leave him—not without seeing his favourite collection of patterns of people.

Oh dear no, he will show you that, never fear, whether you like it or not."

Kovor and Thobrusk exchanged amused and knowing glances.

"So you really came to Kew just to add to your collections?" Brid asked Kovor, just to make sure.

"That is right, but not that only. It all began when the Molk himself first heard your world. He heard it first, you know. It was the world that he knew we would all come to hear, that he warned us would play the great tune and the new music that would call to all Maboria. It tempted us to grow a bridging tree up to the gate that opened the way into your world, that whispered to us so mistily and strange. Once we heard your world singing, we reached out our fingers because we wanted to touch. We could no longer be at peace with ourselves. So some of us came, riding our beasts over the bridging tree, hoping to find new Time, hoping to grow new instruments on which we could play, to capture new expressions and fresh peculiarities, to listen to new blossoms, to taste your breeze, to feel the heart of your birds beat on the wing. The Molkeza wanted—how she wanted—to swim in the air and to *be* in this new world."

"But how did you know it was the way in?" Alex asked curiously. "How did you grow the bridge? What did it bridge over, and where did it reach to?"

Kovor shook his head sadly.

"Ask the Ludaz. I do not know. The Ludaz planted the tree and enticed it to bridge with an Ignet Seed. Uta—she never makes a mistake, you know—drew up the charts of time. For that is what our bridge reached over. It was a movement through time rather than space, and we crossed on our feet and the feet of our beasts. At the far end there was a Gate and a thousand of us came and rode over and through and brought our things with us. The Gate is still there, as shut as ever, as you will see. For we shall pass it on the way to whatever else we are going to look at, I think."

They had been walking by tall, stern trees of holly standing like giant sentries with their dark, spiked leaves. For the first time since the twins had arrived, the sun had gone behind a cloud and the bird-song seemed to have died away. A breeze touched and rustled Thobrusk's feathers. Alex saw his fingers tighten round his staff. He seemed to be looking anywhere but where they were. Suddenly, walking between the two Maborians with their painted feet and their old-young faces, Alex felt how strange they were; and yet as he walked with them, it was as if he had crossed a barrier. Strange they might be, yet he was over on their side. He looked through their eyes when he looked at Kew.

It was almost cold.

"What's that?" Alex cried suddenly.

It was a kind of grumbling rumble. There was the sound of big sticks breaking under a great weight.

"One of the beasts!" Kovor exclaimed.

But Thobrusk was looking at the twins with interest.

"You can hear it?" he inquired. "Quite clearly?"

There was an ear-splitting roar. Brid jumped.

"What *is* it?" she gasped.

"You never heard it before when you came to the Gardens," Thobrusk reminded her. "But the beasts have always been here. We have about two hundred of them."

"Hold my hand now," Kovor commanded. "You have never seen them before either. It is used to them first that you must become."

"But I *have* seen it before," Alex exclaimed. "It's a Kylin, only it's a real live one. There are two stone ones by the Pond near the Palm House."

It was like a cross between a dog, a lion and a bull, a hugely built and powerful animal about the size of a small car, with a mane, and enormous paws; and it was advancing and snarling. A square animal, Alex thought. It rushed loudly towards them in full-force furious attack.

Brid shrank, she couldn't help it. Kovor held her fast.

Thobrusk gazed at the charging animal. He lifted his staff—just a little way.

"Sit down, Afghar," he said softly.

The dog stopped. It was still roaring, still terrible, a great mustard-yellow tongue frothing over its fangs.

Suddenly Thobrusk's staff threatened, his voice rang loud and clear with great authority. "AFGHAR! AFGHAR! YOU WILL BECOME AGAIN WHAT YOU ONCE WERE." Thobrusk was angry.

The Kylin shut its mouth. It bowed its head. It fawned. It squeaked like a castle gate.

"I should think so, Afghar," Thobrusk continued quietly. "Before a lady too. You know I will not have this sort of thing. A quite unnecessary demonstration. Come to the lady for a pat that you simply don't deserve."

There was another grating squeak.

It came close to them. It whimpered. It grovelled on its paws. Its heavy thick tail, like an overgrown fly-whisk, beat the ground in ecstasy. It *purred.*

Rather cautiously, Brid put out a hand. She patted the shaggy head. When she touched the brute the hair felt silken soft, while he was the colour of golden tweed.

"Why, he's gorgeous," Brid said.

"What was it you meant, Sir?" Alex asked, touching the beast gingerly.

"It does not matter. I simply reminded him of old and future Maboria," Thobrusk explained. "That is the time when the Kylins were and will be cubs, when we tame them on the other side of the ring. It is largely forgotten about at this stage for that is many hundreds of years away—but these Kylins, they have better memories than us. Afghar knows what I mean. It was I who trained him, you see. He's brilliant—but he's often bad."

The twins both felt vaguely uncomfortable with the huge beast padding along behind them and so close, snuffling and hissing like some heavy ancient engine. Brid kept looking round. But the Maborians seemed quite at ease.

"The important thing," Thobrusk explained, "is that he should recognize you. Once he knows who you are, there is nothing to worry about."

"And you ride animals like that?" Alex asked.

"When you need a good friend in a difficult country," Thobrusk assured him, "you can be very glad you are astride one of these."

Brid was not at all sure that she fancied riding one of *them.*

"There is the Gateway, up there on the left," Kovor pointed out. "Up on the mound, see."

Alex was suddenly overwhelmed by a tremendous sense of certainty. He had seen this Gateway before, of course, with Uncle Frederick, who had pointed out to them how it was beautifully and strangely made with carvings of dragons, with copper and fretted shapes and faces. It was a queer Gate that stood by itself under its own thatched roof. It did not lead anywhere. It did not shut anybody out of anywhere. You could walk right round it and it was always closed. It too had Kylins carved on it—but of course it would. He now knew why the Gate was there. It was the Maborians' way in, the way from another world.

They climbed the mound, the Gateway stood above them, large, larger than themselves, and yet somehow *small*—as if it had been made for something else.

"The Gate will not open now," Kovor was explaining. "If we were to use force it would only shatter and then, what would we see? Why, the other side of the mound only. You do not go *through* the Gate that way."

At that moment Afghar bounded away from them, uttering a sudden and surprising high-pitched whining noise. He snuffled heavily up to the massive gates and lifting a big paw, he dabbed at them, crying sorrowfully. He nosed back and forth at the Gate, pushing with his paw at the stout bar that closed it.

"What's the matter with him?" Brid asked.

Thobrusk was watching with careful attention.

"He remembers that the Gate was our way in," he

said. "Afghar was one of the first to come through. He remembers Maboria—it is his homeland, just as it is mine."

Thobrusk tapped his staff. The Kylin sobbed again and then crept back to his master, crouching and huge above him.

"But why can't you open the Gate?" Alex insisted. "It doesn't look too difficult to me. You've only to lift that bar."

"Because," Kovor explained, "it is more difficult than you imagine. How we have tried! The lock is more cunning, more wonderful than one can dream of. My key will not work here, Alex. Again and again we have forged other keys—uttered passwords, made signs and played secret music. The Molkeza has even sung to it. It only became tighter. Exasperating, it was."

"But you can see light through at the top," Alex pointed out.

"Yes," Thobrusk agreed. "You can see the light—and if you were to climb up and look, all that you would see would be Kew Gardens on the other side. . . ."

But while they were talking, Brid had slipped quietly in under the roof of the Gate. It was up to her and Alex to help the Maborians and their Kylins home. The bar seemed to be perfectly simple to her. She slid it neatly to one side. It moved easily. She pushed. She pulled. With just a little creak the gates moved.

WHEEEEEEE!

Like a terrible fist, they were hit by a wind like a wall—a hurricane roaring and raging through the open Gateway and Brid was tottering on an *edge*—

held back only by the wind—the very edge of bottomless cliff—nothing but cloud marching and hurricane howling and cold distance and the whirling black abyss of falling nothingness over the edge of unimagined Time.

"The Bridge," Kovor cried, "the Bridge, our Bridge home, it is no longer there."

"Brid!" Alex yelled in a desperate warning, and his voice seemed so small and snatched away.

Only by the wind . . . if she took one more step . . . Kovor struggled forward but could not. The wind screamed and screeched through the Gateway. Alex was hurled sprawling. Brid herself—her hair blown against her face—did not know how close . . .

There was only Thobrusk . . .

"AFGHAR, AFGHAR, remember what you do!"

. . . and then the Kylin, a Kylin of Maboria, flung himself at the teeth of the wind with a great spring, had seized Brid, her dress in his jaws, and with a massive pull of the great shoulders she was dragged back . . .

Of themselves the Gates clanged shut.

There was silence.

Even Afghar was silent, the girl safe in his jaws. He laid her very softly on the grass. Alex sat dazed. Thobrusk, still standing, stared without speech across the quiet Gardens, the motionless trees, the still, unmoving leaves.

It was Kovor who first ran to Brid. Her eyes were open. She lay bewildered.

"Untouched," he gasped. "By Olbaboth it is all right that you feel? It is not forgiving myself that I'll be."

She smiled. "Tell me. What happened?"

And then they all heard Thobrusk. He was speaking as if to himself. He was speaking far away; remembering, understanding and expecting.

"We have seen the Gates re-open and there was nothing but the great Gulf. We knew that the winds of Time blew always and that nothing lasts for long before their blowing. Now we have seen indeed that they have swept our bridge away, yet still we have to cross that Gulf, if we are ever going to come once more to our Maboria."

CHAPTER NINE

It seemed almost impossible to imagine that anything extraordinary had happened. The birds twittered, the sun came out once more. It was very peaceful under the trees. Afghar had wrapped his nose in his paws and had gone to sleep.

But Alex could still feel himself shaking. He was not sure if it was because he was afraid or because he was . . . excited. He only knew that he had seen—OUT, out through that Gateway, out—otherwards, across Time. But into what?

"Is my skirt straight at the back, Alex?" Brid was asking him. She did nothing but straighten herself up. She had borrowed his comb. Kovor had charmed her by producing a mirror.

"For adjusting the feathers, you know. I always carry one."

But Alex knew Brid just didn't bother about being

tidy. It was only when something was troubling her that she would start it. He felt troubled himself.

Thobrusk still stared into the far distance.

Kovor sat in his yellow feathers, his chin to his knees, waiting patiently.

Alex sat down too and then got up again. He felt very shuddery.

"You need not be ashamed of feeling afraid." It was as if Thobrusk's serene voice was sounding right in the middle of his mind. Alex stopped shaking.

"We are all afraid when we look out and down and up into the Gulf of Time, when we hang suspended on the lip of nothing, when we look out over the grey chasm that still lies between the now, the then and the shall-be. We are afraid, but we are also wiser. Sometimes, Alex, it is good to do the terrifying thing—to look into its face and still not turn away."

"But it does lead somewhere too. I mean you Maborians travel over it."

Thobrusk looked down at him.

"Exactly, Alex. That is precisely what you have to remember. The Gulf is not just something to fall forever into—it is also what you travel over. Indeed, it is what connects us to Maboria. When we can remember that, we need not be quite so afraid."

Thobrusk's words were comforting.

"But what I still don't understand," Alex confessed, "is how we can help you to cross the Gulf. I mean we're only Brid and me."

"Come, come," Thobrusk replied, "only Brid and you. Have you not shown that when you bring your time into contact with ours, remarkable things happen? And have you not at last seen the beasts who have always been here, the clouds that have always swirled beyond the Gate? Remember how few there are who can see Maborians at all. You may not be impressed by what you have shown that you can do today, but we Maborians are."

Alex thought about this. "But I still don't quite see," he said finally, "how it all adds up. You see, we didn't have to try very hard."

"Precisely," Thobrusk agreed. "You succeeded in your unexpected results perhaps for that very reason. But at the moment you are, I suspect, trying very hard indeed, trying desperately to understand what it is that you will have to do, where you are going, everything?" Thobrusk looked deeply at Alex in his amused yet serious way.

"Well, yes," Alex admitted sheepishly.

"Well, don't," Thobrusk advised simply. "Be content just to taste, to see shapes and colours, to listen and hear sounds. Put out your fingers and feel the hot and the cold, the rough and the smooth. Isn't that really enough?"

"Well, yes," Alex admitted again, smiling back at Thobrusk, "I suppose so."

"It is quite enough that you two have talked," Kovor chimed in. "We should be moving on, otherwise we shall not be reaching the next thing. Madam Brid need not worry herself a scrap about it, because I shall be in charge and I know exactly what will happen, and you two will only have to watch and worth watching it will be, as Thobrusk knows."

Thobrusk nodded again.

Brid had finished combing her hair. In spite of it all, Afghar had been very gentle. She had taken off her sandals and knocked out the dirt. (A good thing she had not been wearing her tights, she thought.) She handed Kovor back his mirror—it was triangular, a polished metal, not glass at all.

"Where are you taking us to, Kovor?" she asked.

"I am taking you up," he replied. "Up the Pagoda."

"The Pagoda?" Brid exclaimed—all nervousness immediately forgotten.

"At last. We always wanted to go in," Alex said. "What's it like inside? What do you find at the top?"

"To see what is at the top is why we are going there," Kovor told them and all at once he was leading the way.

The Pagoda stood tall and red in the centre of the green grass. Surrounding it, at a respectful distance, the trees rose too, swaying a little in the breeze and nothing like so high. The Pagoda's roofs were in layers like hats, balanced one above the other—ten brims—ten hats rising. Under these roofs it was red, the walls were bricks of red, at the bottom there were two red doors.

Kovor produced his large key and of course it opened the door. As soon as they slipped in, he closed it again and relocked it. Afghar followed them up to the door—he grunted once or twice—mewed—and then sat down on guard.

There was nothing to be seen on the ground floor except the wooden staircase winding upward and upward and a long carved wooden chest against the wall.

"But before you start there is a condition," Kovor began quickly. "Nothing is easy and this is more difficult. Before you go further you must take off your shoes, as Maborians do not wear them, and put on feathers because Maborians do. That is because, and the why of it is—that unless you can both look and feel as a Maborian looks and a Maborian feels, you will not see and hear and know when you reach the highest floor. Afterwards, when you come down again, then you must change back. For you will not be able to open our way home for us unless you are yourselves."

"If you can bear it just for a moment," Thobrusk added quietly.

"Do you mean you want us to change into feathers?" Brid asked eagerly. "Feathers like yours."

Kovor was nodding.

Perhaps we shall have to grow them, Alex thought suddenly.

"Yes and no," Thobrusk replied out loud as he opened the chest. Inside the lid there was a mirror, a polished metal mirror, and within the chest there lay clumps of feathers, three, four or five of them, all a rich and earthy brown. The twins supposed that they were sort of cloaks, but they had no proper shape.

They were fascinated to see Thobrusk lifting the first one out—for the feathers were in a way separate, they poured into Thobrusk's hands like a liquid, and yet each feather clung to its neighbour and did not fall away while the whole shape of the clump changed, like a cloud, like a net, feathers magnetized one to the other, flitting and moving and alive.

"You will find," Thobrusk explained, "that there are no fastenings. It will come together of itself. It has no shape except the shape you are. It will always fit."

Thobrusk stood there gravely pouring the tiny tawny-brown feathers from one hand to the other.

"But how do you begin?" Alex asked, his eyes trying to follow every feather. "I mean, there are no sleeves. There doesn't seem to be a hole to put your head through."

Thobrusk nodded.

"You just take off your things and then tip the feathers over one shoulder. You will find that they will cling to you."

"And to wear them will be the moment that you become one of us," Kovor added. "That moment will be a privilege for all Maboria and grateful we will be and favour we shall have."

He looked at them anxiously, as if afraid that even now they might refuse.

But the twins were not even listening. Already they felt the wooden boards under their bare feet, they had put their sandals down in a row. Alex was taking his sweater off over his head, Brid was folding up her skirt and Kovor found himself putting their things away for them in the chest. Brid held her breath as Thobrusk poured a chestnut cloak of feathers over her bare shoulder . . .

. . . and she was dressed, she was brown with feathers. It was like wearing both less and more. It was so light, and then she was spread with a glow of warmth, yet she felt as free as if wearing nothing at all. She just wanted to jump.

She was distracted by seeing Thobrusk do the same for Alex. He brother stood there all pale. Last year's sun-tan had almost gone. And then with a certain shiver the feathers came pouring over his shoulder, a whispering rush and the brownness cascaded down on all sides of him, down his arms almost to the elbow, round him like a shirt and shorts at once, sleek and tight as those of Corbrey himself.

"I say," Alex said. Then: "I'll race you up to the top, two at a time. Can we go?"

But Kovor led them. The stairs went round and round. Kovor did not run, and yet they did not stop or look out of the windows on the way. Brid got an accidental glimpse of trees once, but they kept onwards and upwards. It was a long way. Much further than it had seemed from the ground. Even in their feathers they began to feel puffed.

"Now we are half-way up and it's already twice as far as one wants to go," Kovor declared. "You can always tell because this is where Harragong's portrait is. She keeps it there to remind everyone that she can run all the way up to the top without stopping or getting out of breath. She is the only one of us who can do it, you see."

On the next turn of the stair, there was a large dark picture in an elaborately carved and gilded frame—of Harragong indeed, but Harragong astride a red-eyed Kylin galloping, with a long net in one hand, and she was swinging it above her head.

"She is hunting the Ignet Seed and that is Umbrij she is riding, who is the most alarming Kylin that we have, much fiercer than Afghar. Harragong is the only one of us who can manage him," Kovor explained.

"What's an Ignet Seed?" Brid asked, trying hard to identify one in the picture.

"An Ignet Seed? Well you may ask, Brid, for you

will be meeting one soon. The Seed is a beginning, our beginning—the only kind of beginning we can know. We who are immortal have no beginnings of our own. We have to have them grown and then we hunt them for ourselves as Ignet Seeds. Harragong is the best huntress we have. They travel fast, you know."

Alex stared at the now familiar face of the Molkeza with a new respect. He was certain he could not ride a Kylin like that. Her long hair was streaming out behind her in the wind, she gripped the animal with her bare brown knees, she rode without saddle or bridle, and there was a glitter in her eye.

"We must keep going," Kovor reminded them. "Up we go, or we shall not reach the top and only from there shall we see what we shall hear."

"You catch the Ignet Seed with a net?" Alex asked.

"The Molkeza does," Thobrusk agreed. "She is the only one of us who quite succeeds—at speed."

At last, at long last, Brid thought, they were reaching the top. Kovor led them out, out through a door and on to the highest gallery.

"But whatever you do, don't look down," he warned them. "To look down is to look back, to look back is not to see what is to come. Look up Brid, look up Alex, and outward and straight ahead—and tell me what you see."

"I can see the clouds again," Alex said gazing out, a slight tinge of anxiety in his voice, "like we saw through the Gate."

And there were the huge grey clouds piling and curling, angered and ragged. They raced against and over and under each other, majestic like tall ships scudding before a storm, endless and voyaging. Alex was uneasy in spite of himself. But there was a difference from the view through the Gate. Here, on the topmost gallery of the Pagoda, it was warm. And Brid seemed happy and not a breath of wind touched their faces.

Again Kovor murmured in their ears:

"For here the Pagoda is not what it seems. Here we are on a mast reaching upwards through Time towards Maboria. Here we can watch across the great gulfs and in the distance we may still hear and see and call towards that which is Maberdy, the world that is Maboria. From here over distance we see the space of time. So too we overheard your world, far away whispering, now nearer, now further—oh, wonderful it was when we heard, Alex. Oh, Brid, how we wanted to come! But now it is our home that sometimes we hear singing . . ."

Kovor gazed upwards and outwards. From under his yellow feathers he produced a row of tiny silver pipes, and then he looked round at the twins, suddenly less serious, and he grinned.

"I shall not sing until I have regained my harp. But that does not mean that Kovor will not play his pipes—and if I play, then Time itself will listen with its ears."

Brid and Alex felt Thobrusk take their hands and then they heard Kovor's first note that came forward softly otherward, a shy note to be followed, shadowed, a note tempting, laughing a little, lurking by another, by a whole shoal like scarlet fishes swimming, flitting—silence. New notes now pleading, asking, piercing, and so sad, so sad, so far away. Now

Kovor's piping rising, travelling, leaving, and the grey clouds rolling, blotting out everything and then again . . . silence.

Thobrusk's hands tightened.

A single mote of sunlight.

There was a voice, not Kovor's voice.

A voice slowly singing.

A voice sang of a tree on a green mountain that could remember old age and looked forward, how long it looked forward, to the time when it was young. It sang to a harp, to strings plucked in immensity, a questing sound, gentle and searchful.

"Flothba," Kovor whispered. "Flothba sings still across Maboria."

"It is Flothba's song," Thobrusk echoed. "Listen, do you hear?"

The twins heard. They heard the Maborian voice, remembering what he once had known and looking forward to where the water fell under the high towers of Maberdy.

And as he sang. . . . "Look," Brid whispered.

Kovor and Thobrusk saw that they heard and knew that they could see. Hearing and seeing became one thing.

The clouds were falling away and it was like looking towards another horizon, a horizon that was approaching them.

"Maboria," Alex replied. It was like a brilliant stain, a new colour spreading across his mind, across both their minds.

A grey-blue lagoon sparkled in the arms of a forest and a city, a city of buildings like sails, a forest of archways, a lagoon that reached backward and glided through cloisters; and from windows above them, from high ports and doorways, water frothed downward tumbling in rainbows. Above and beyond them houses rose like masts, belled out with the wind and nodding, spreading blossoms in sunlight and luminous with colour.

And all the while the single voice continued to tell them, that Maboria was waiting, that Maberdy grew otherward to prepare for their coming, their returning, their arrival, their joining if only . . . and then receded.

Again Kovor played back, played back on the silver pipes, a glee jig, an excitement, a dance in the hay-loft.

Alex could see a boat darting over the lagoon's surface, a jewel in a bubble, quivering in moment. Brid watched feathered people, feathered as she was, gathering in a hallway and waving; and Maberdy became twilit with dotted lamps and the voice of Flothba became fainter and Time returned with its spaces and cloud, surly and grumbling.

Alex fought back his unease as the distance increased again, as cloud rose on cloud, as space stretched outward into space, time lengthened outward into time.

"Come away. Come back. You must come now—while you may," Kovor urged.

Still the twins stood on the gallery in their feathers and in contrast the air suddenly seemed chill on their bare legs. Now there was only the sense of endless distance, that distance that they would have to cross and cover if ever their friends were to return to the lagoon, to the sailing city.

Yet space, time and distance were in their heads and stained by all the colours of Maboria.

Brid felt the soft brown feathers that went over her, she felt them shiver, she felt them with her hands.

"I don't feel we have earned them yet," she whispered, looking at Alex.

"But we shall," Alex whispered back, and then added thoughtfully as he remembered Thobrusk's words, "I think we may even be beginning to now."

There was another deeper whisper behind them.

"Oh sir, oh madam, the moment has come for the launching of an Ignet Seed: the Molkeza is summoning you, at once and at your pleasure and without doubt, to her part of the programme."

Thobrusk and Kovor were standing to one side. Corbrey was bowing to the floor.

CHAPTER TEN

It was hot—green and heavily hot. It had been a rush to get here, down all the Pagoda stairs, with a quick stop to change back into their ordinary things—and the greenhouse, where Harragong was, *had* to be right up the other end of Kew Gardens. Corbrey had urged them on with terrible whispers. (Kovor had defended them. "Can't you see they're doing the best they can?") The grey and dusty Thobrusk remained unflustered, most helpful and practically silent. Brid was wishing she could have stayed in her cool, floating costume of feathers. Alex just felt hot.

On the way they had passed a small crowd of Maborians gathered by the path round a large urn in which an instrument was growing, was thrusting out with many tiny horns. The Maborien among them was touching it with her small fingers and the plant sang—Brid and Alex had only just been able to hear it—a whirring, droning song that sank away when she removed her hand. Kovor had waved a greeting as they strode by.

At last they all came round a hedge, just by a clump of orange roses and they had arrived at quite a small glasshouse set back all by itself. Corbrey had led the way up the steps.

"This way please, Brid—Alex," he whispered. "Here we must leave you now. Just go through these doors and close them behind you, and then through the further pair. The Molkeza is beyond them."

"And good luck to you too, that you shall need and shall have," Kovor added.

Thobrusk's eyes twinkled.

They had gone inside alone. It was very hot indeed. For an instant they paused. They both realized that though their feet had brought them here, most of them still seemed left behind, seemed to be on the Pagoda's topmost gallery. The colours and the sounds were still splashed right through their heads. But even as they paused they heard a voice, another far more familiar voice singing. It sang very loudly and very, very badly in the unmistakable and irascible tones of Harragong.

It was accompanied by a very noisy and rhythmic sound of sloshing water. Suddenly the singing stopped.

"I knew that you both had a real need to be alone," Harragong called through the door. "And you'll certainly never have any peace with that lot out there. That's why I'm inviting you in here for a bit of real peace and quiet with me."

A little rivulet of hot water oozed out from under her door and ran over Brid's foot. Brid started back.

"I should think she's launched an Ignet Seed already," Alex whispered in an undertone.

"Nonsense! You can't possibly *think* properly unless you first RELAX," the voice came again. "Both my ears grow on the sides of my head. They can hear. They can hear you. Come on IN. You may as well make a pleasure out of doing what Harragong tells you to do—and volunteer for it. Come and see me make the clicking Ignet Plant release a seed. It's the most relaxing thing in the world."

The twins weren't so certain that they did want to relax with Harragong exactly, but she was the Molkeza and she did seem to be insisting.

Alex hesitated. It was Brid who opened the door. At first they could hardly see the wood for the steam.

The big glass room was like the edge of a forest with huge fan-like palms and round the edges many melons, loofahs and cucumbers grew. In the middle, in a sort of cross between a swimming pool and a luxury bath, floating at her ease in the bubbling green water, was the irrepressible Harragong.

"Helloo," the Molkeza called with enormous zest.

"Hello," Alex and Brid replied, rather cautiously.

There were tiny purple flowers growing in her bath water and festoons of snow-white blossoms arching overhead. Golden fish swam in the water with her, round-eyed and blowing. In the background a gigantic water plant grew up and out of the pool, a mass of long and curling silver leaves,

leaves with spikes and points like sharp-nailed fingers, stalks with daggers drawn. The twins could just make out a huge spear-shaped pod, a silvered seed pod guarded by the hundred prickling hiding leaves. In here no breeze blew and yet the huge plant swayed, backwards and forwards, forwards and backwards, patient as a watching clock.

In the middle of everything floated the Molkeza, a large bath sponge in one hand, a long green butterfly net in the other. Near by, on a lily leaf, was a cube of pinkest soap and her bath salts tanged the air.

"That's right—I wash at the same time," Harragong explained conversationally. "I couldn't possibly waste having to be in all this hot water."

She duck-dived under the surface and now they could see her swimming like an otter, her long black hair streaming out behind her. Then she vanished and disappeared for almost a minute.

Brid began to get quite anxious until there she was again with a kind of explosive gasp, only to dive once more, feet kicking strongly.

"What *is* she doing?" Alex asked. He had always wanted to be able to swim in his bath.

"What am I doing?" Harragong repeated, surfacing behind him and flicking back her black, wet hair with an expert jerk of her head. "I am suggesting to this Ignet Plant that it might release a seed."

She waved up towards the spiked plant that was swaying slowly above their heads.

"An Ignet is a water plant, a ticking tocking clocking plant, while its seed is a flying, gliding, moving seed. The plant sways east and west and the seed flies high and wide and you have to persuade the first to give up the last. They are spiky, parachuting, independent things, that don't like being made to give and don't like being told what to do, and I start 'em, entice 'em and tell 'em."

"Have you started this one yet?" Brid inquired, her eyes following the to and fro of the watching Ignet Plant. She was glad that she hadn't got to ask it any favours.

Harragong, who had gradually been re-submerging, re-emerged.

"Started it? I haven't even tried to start it yet. I have only been entertaining it." She pushed the hair out of her eyes once more and grinned. "We Maborians must amuse and know and trust the plants with which we live. We have to tease even our own homes to open up and let us in. We have to smile at the chanting tree, the flower that sounds our song. We must be courteous to the leaf that breathes and floats and carries us through lofty halls, the long lagoons of our Maboria. So the Ignet plant has really got to LIKE me first before it will release the seed: that's why I'm entertaining it.

"You see," the Molkeza continued cheerfully, "I'm THE entertainer of Maboria. I cheer up a wilted weed."

WHOOSH—and she was entertaining her Ignet Plant, speeding round and round, zig-zagging, diving, twirling and twisting, somersaulting under water, feet threshing—out of sight, her path marked only by a line of streaking bubbles and by her net that whipped like a periscope above the surface. A huge bow wave swished round the pool and broke in spray against the side.

"I'm wet!" cried Brid indignantly and then grinned hurriedly.

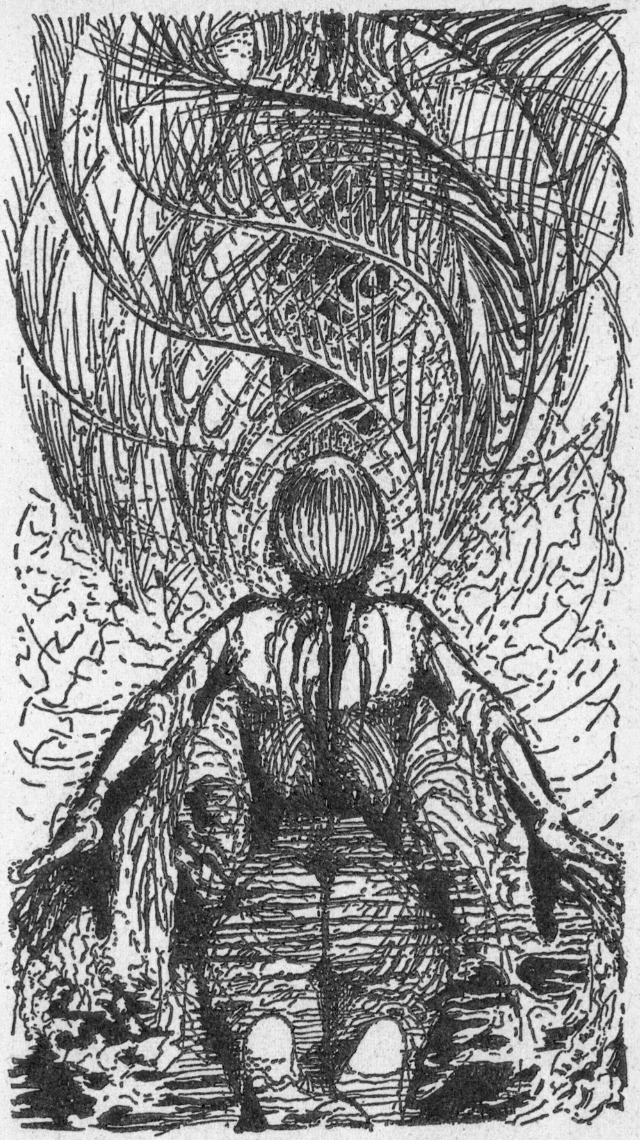

"You're not as wet as me," Harragong chuckled from the other side. "You see, if I didn't make a splash, it wouldn't even notice me." She floated towards them now, just floating among the leaves and under the arching palms. "Watch it," she whispered to them over the shimmering water. "How fast it sways. Do you see the inside of the silver leaves? They're orange and they're green, they're dark blue and they're umbcr, they're all the colours of Maboria. It always shows its colours when it's interested."

Eagerly they leaned further out over the water. It was so hot in here that it hardly mattered how wet you got anyway. They gazed, fascinated, at the gyrating, glinting leaves.

Harragong trod water. The green waves flowed over her black shoulders. She put her tongue between her white teeth and watched them watch. Her laugh was as deep as the water in which she swam.

"You are watching," she explained—flicking drops of hot water with some accuracy so that they only just missed first one twin and then the other—"you are watching the beginning of a start. It is something that I have always grown. The others are always collecting things that *are*. I grow something that is *new*. The start is the plant with the seed. That's fun. Then I let the seed escape. That's more fun still. Then Harragong goes hunting. Then we all go hunting to find a new beginning."

Harragong glanced up anxiously at her Ignet Plant which was now slowing to its original and gentle rhythm. She wiggled one of her silver toes in its direction, she clapped her hands. She conducted it with her butterfly net.

"Come ON," Harragong insisted.

Hesitantly, and then more confidently, the Ignet Plant responded and the sway of the leaves began to quicken.

Satisfied, Harragong returned to the twins. She put her butterfly net over her head and then peered at Alex through the mesh. She seemed to like the experiment because she then peered at Brid. It was as if she was now wearing a thinking cap.

Once again Alex felt that he was being invited to read her thoughts.

"We—" he began. "Brid and I—do *we* have to have a new beginning in all this?"

Harragong doffed her butterfly net in deep acknowledgement.

"That is exactly and completely and twice over the point of the programme here. We are growing you a new beginning of your own. You see, we needed an Ignet Seed to open up the bridge towards your world. So we think you'll need a new beginning too, to open up the way to ours."

Excitedly the Molkeza somersaulted underwater two or three times, stopped, raised a dark arm towards a loofah growing overhead, picked it and then looked hopefully at the twins.

"So when this Seed escapes, YOU will have to do the catching. That's your part of the programme. The Ignet Seed will be yours for the chasing."

"But you'll be here to help us hunt it, won't you, Harragong?" Brid asked anxiously, thinking of that picture on the Pagoda stairs.

"Oh, I'll be here all right," Harragong chuckled, "but *I'm* only going to watch. Unless you catch it for yourselves, it won't be yours."

SCLOOSH!

Harragong returned to entertaining in earnest. She was like a mosquito hovering, a propeller spinning, a firefly in darting water—and she was gone, had reappeared, here she was, there she was. . . . Now the green water swirled round and round, and Alex and Brid got wetter and wetter and the leaves of the Plant swayed faster and faster. Colours flashed and the twins were dazzled—and click, click, click, they could even hear it now. Swaying—no, it wasn't just swaying, it was actually turning, the hundred curling points weaving in on themselves: always silver, but blue against orange and green against umber.

Brid watched.

Alex watched.

Harragong was dancing for her Ignet Plant and the Ignet Plant, wonderfully delighted, was dancing for Harragong.

Suddenly the Molkeza stopped still.

"It's getting too excited, too wound up," she called, and threw her butterfly net at Alex. "Here, grab this—you'll need it when the Seed escapes."

Alex caught it. It was twice as heavy as he expected.

Brid was feeling dizzy herself. She sat down but still couldn't take her eyes off the frenzied, whirling Ignet Plant and this made her feel worse. If the Plant could move like this, what sort of dance would the Seed give them? Brid's heart began to sink.

"Easy there, my beauty," Harragong was warning it. "You'll do something terrible in a minute. Aren't you a simply splendid plant? How about slowing down a bit so that we can see you?" She grabbed at the nearest leaves and smiled as it struggled.

Harragong was strong. She could have thrown an oak. Her brown hands hung on until the whirling ceased. In a final burst the Ignet Plant inflated all its spiky leaves as though in anger, but then thought better of it, as the Molkeza laughingly let go.

The click, click, click, had stopped. But the Plant began to purr, a hoarsely grating, affectionate sort of noise. And now it was laying down its pointed leaves like thin shafts of silver fanning out, exposing the whole of the seed-pod that rose magnificently from its centre. The pod was exquisite, perfect, tall and spear-shaped, the silver casing deeply engraved with a thousand slender lines. By concentrating hard, the twins could just make out that the lines were deepening all the time.

"That's it, my splendour!" cried the Molkeza excitedly. "You're Harragong's, aren't you my wonder? That's being the best. Come on—come on you lovely thing—you like me, don't you?"

Suddenly the slender lines turned into holes. The pod was swelling rapidly and now it was a sphere of silver strings, tightening, turning and twisting into a vibrating shimmering cage.

Harragong splashed up and down in encouragement.

"Better! Better! You sunflower. You orchid. NO! NO! You weed in the flowerbed you, you'll never do. AHH! That's it, my rose in morning glory. That's it. You took far too long—but I still love you."

The sphere, the cage, the strings, all became still.

The twins remembered Corbrey and his cage of

time, the cage they had destroyed. Now they had seen one made.

"There's something inside," Brid whispered, a little awe-inspired.

Now there was a distant humming sound coming from inside the cage. They could see a scarlet light within the silver threads, a light struggling, floundering, attempting to escape.

"The Seed," Alex whispered. "The beginning of our beginning."

"And when it escapes," Harragong said triumphantly, "and escape it will, then you will have the new beginning that you can hunt for yourselves and make your own. Remember, until you capture it, it is not yours!" She swam backwards and away, a powerful backstroke with a flurry of silver toes and beating feet. The time cage shuddered. The scarlet light brightened, enlarged and grew. The hum rose in pitch.

"It's opening," Brid whispered, one hand on her brother's wrist. She began to chew the nails of her free hand.

How could they ever catch it, if even Harragong needed to ride a Kylin, if the Seed could keep ahead of her when she never ran out of breath, if she was always so fast? What could they do? But there wasn't time now even to think, they could only look and it was so queer, so weird. The silver strings shone white. They stretched and tightened. There was a kind of shuddering growth. What was within was emerging, coming out into the daylight like a red wig on a stalk, like a scarlet furry parachute.

"It's an EXPLOSION," Harragong called.

For an instant Brid and Alex saw each other, pale

and white in the heat. They saw the Molkeza treading water among the lily leaves. They saw the Seed rise. It began to open and open over the pool, like a huge umbrella, and as it unfolded, it grew. It brushed the creepers, the overhanging palms; it almost seemed to clutch. Alex felt himself wanting to duck, to hide away, to go back into a corner. But he lifted the net. The Seed was getting bigger and bigger.

"It will go through the roof," Harragong warned them from the far side of the pool. "Then you can begin your hunt—IF YOU DARE."

The Seed had dropped. It rose. It bumped against the glass. There was a hissing bubbling sound. It was swelling and inflating....

The Molkeza was still backing away, waist deep in the water, watching them, half anxious, half smiling.

"Go outside," she shouted. "GO OUTSIDE. You may catch it floating down from the roof."

But the twins did not go outside. They reached up, instinctively, as if there was nothing else they could do. They stretched out. Alex stretched out his net.

Afterwards, when they had thought very hard, they had both said: "There was a sort of colour, a scent that hung in your head." It had been neither a bright colour nor a very strong scent. And then they had remembered that brighter stain and stronger colour that they had seen from the Pagoda so short a time ago, that had touched the insides of their minds. This was a paler, quieter version here, yet this had made them act. It happened so quickly. They simply stretched up their hands, stretched up their net. It was Brid who spoke in her ordinary, usual, conversational voice:

"We need you. Please come down."

"It'll be AWAY," Harragong cried from the far end.

But it did nothing of the sort. Very slowly and unhurriedly and very patiently, the Ignet Seed sank down. It shrank. It lowered itself carefully into Alex's waiting net. Its light went out. The hissing died away. It folded. Brid reached down to touch it. It became smaller. She picked it out, and passed it to Alex. He took it—it was vanishing into a small ball of fur—he dropped the net and the Seed was between his hands, it was warm. Brid took it between hers. There was no struggle. They turned round.

Harragong had climbed out of the pool. She stood there, holding a towel of white swansdown, and gazing at them rather blankly, almost as if she could not quite believe her eyes. In a very little voice she said:

"Are you quite sure it's safe?"

The twins nodded breathlessly.

"You are—you are quite, quite sure?"

"Yes," they said together, knowing that they were right though hardly knowing why.

There was an absolute silence except for the lapping of the water in the pool.

"Well," said Brid with a hint of pride in her voice, "we've caught it."

Harragong, Molkeza of all Maboria and Archmaborien, could only nod.

"Have we done the wrong thing?" Alex asked, suddenly anxious.

The Molkeza shook her head. Then she managed to find her voice again, but it was still rather small.

"It was such a powerful Seed. I can't remember having seen one caught without a chase before. You haven't just caught a new beginning. You *are* a new beginning! What a birthday!"

"But what must we do with the Seed, Harragong?" Brid asked.

The Molkeza blinked. Then very carefully she tied her feather towel about her middle, screwed her long black hair into a wet black rope which she squeezed—and then she laughed.

"DO with it? You don't have to do anything with it. You've got it. Now you care for it. Wrap it up when it's cold. Fan it in the sunshine. Be kind to it. Maybe it will be kind to you—then maybe, it'll decide to DO something for you."

The door was opening behind them. It was Thobrusk standing there, as usual in his dusty feathers, tall and calm. He bowed, very gravely, in their direction. Then he smiled.

"The wine. It is the taste of the wine. It has changed significantly today. There is a silver sparkle in the glass. We are nearing, I think, the climax of the programme. The Molk himself awaits our guests. May they come now?"

"What did I say?" Harragong declared, fully recovered. "The end of the programme, but the beginning of a beginning. Of course you must go to the Molk—though he'll insist on showing you his collection as well. Dear Moli—still, his *is* simply marvellous. But don't forget—whatever you do, look after your Ignet Seed."

CHAPTER ELEVEN

A little triumphantly but very carefully, they were carrying their Ignet Seed. Brid put out a tentative finger and stroked the bright shining fur. It snuggled comfortably in the palm of Alex's hand.

"This way," Thobrusk said. "I am taking you straight to the Molk's own growing room." He gave a dry smile. "In there things are unusual, as perhaps you know."

They were walking down an aisle between high banks of tall plants with spotted leaves, long twisted slotted leaves with crimson-dotted flowers, long trumpet-yellow flowers, waxy staring bending flowers.

The twins picked their way across the puddles. It was steamier than ever here. Thobrusk opened another door and closed it for them after they had passed through.

"So here you are," came the deep and familiar voice. "Come in Brid, my dear. Come on in, Alex. Come on into my little growing room."

They had entered an immensely long gallery.

Inside it was even hotter and even wetter. There were puddles everywhere. Everything dripped. The Molk stood in the middle, tall and huge and smiling delightedly, wearing a large pair of gumboots. Behind him, as far as the eye could see, green things were growing, were reaching out and hanging down in the steam.

"Whew!" Alex said.

Brid wondered for a moment if she was going to be all right.

"You have to have it warm to make things grow," the Molk remarked. "Warm and wet. The warmer and wetter the bigger and better, I say."

He wiped his brow with an immense hand.

"Some of the others say it's because I spend so much time in here that I'm the size I am. It's not true. I've always been this size. But you'll soon get used to it. Always takes just a minute or four."

He came stumping up towards them.

"So you've caught your own Ignet Seed? That was well done. Very well done. What we'd all hoped for—and that's why I've asked you here. Of course I expect they all told you it was really just so that I could show you my. . . ."

He paused in mid-sentence—he turned to look at a plant just at the level of his right eye—a very tall, reddish, drooping hanging thing—he still paused. Brid forgot to feel uncomfortable. She watched to see what he was going to do.

The Molk jabbed at the soil in the pot with a big finger.

"Everybody will say," he started again, grinning hugely, "that it's only the old Molk's collection. Everybody has to see his collection. It's the biggest —the best collection, they'll say. He shows it to everyone, they'll say. I know."

He patted the reddish plant on the head.

"As a matter of fact," he said confidentially, "*I* think Ludaz has the best collection. Not as large as mine, of course. But his is—well he has—I get the impression that he has got—well it's more brilliant, you know."

"Thobrusk explained a little to us," Brid began. She had rather hoped that the Molk would show them his collection.

The Molk nodded enthusiastically.

"Thobrusk is very wise. You should see his vines. Bunches! Bunches and bunches of velvety purply grapes. He grows flavours. Every year is different. But I don't grow flavours. For me every plant, it's my friend. Sometimes," the Molk added thoughtfully, "my best friend."

He turned round.

"This one for example."

The twins looked.

It was a tall yellow flower with large opening petals.

The twins looked. It was only a flower—a very rich, elaborate flower, incredibly alive, exotic and shining. And then if one looked carefully. . . .

Brid saw. All at once Brid saw.

"It's the man in the antique shop!" she exclaimed.

"That's right," the Molk said, rather pleased. "At least it's his pattern. Of course *he* is his pattern too—even more so. I like him. He sells junk. He's unusual too. I'll tell you something. Sometimes—he can't see the others—but he can see me. Sold me something. Big blue vase. Didn't really need it. But it was fun to buy it off him. You see, we can't often buy things. Your people don't want to see us. Well, I didn't really buy it. Gave him a fir-cone. We swopped. I don't think he really saw anything odd about me. I was rather pleased to work out *his* pattern."

Next to the gay yellow flower was a very small,

tidy, tight-leaved, grey little plant, in a neat little pot, very clean and very trim.

"Now this one's from a little old lady who comes into the Gardens. I often see her although she can't see me. It's made her pattern very well. It was not a difficult one perhaps; older people are so much easier to do. They've stamped themselves *on* themselves, if you follow me."

He turned his little old lady plant round lovingly.

"How do we do it? Well, you could think of it this way. Perhaps you've noticed that in your world, when a man keeps a dog for a long time he begins to *look* like his dog. And not only that—his dog begins to look like him. Now that's a case of patterns swopping over naturally. We just do it with plants and people. More technically perhaps: it needs a lot of attention and takes a long time—but being immortal we've got a long time to do it in—though here in Kew we have to be extra careful about keeping these greenhouses at just the right heat and wetness to make it work. Some of us—like Ludaz and Uta—are almost more fascinated by the actual swopping process, but I prefer to look at the results."

Alex was enjoying the results himself. It was not that the plants looked like people. Nor were they just flowers and leaves that were extremely pretty or fantastic in the usual sense—like Uncle Frederick's carnations and fuchsias. The Molk's collection sat in their pots, low down and clutching themselves, stretching heads pointedly up; or they cascaded themselves, bubbling out of their baskets, blobs of brilliant suspended colour. Each plant was unique, like each face in a crowd. Alex felt that he was surrounded by dozens of characters, all intangible and yet each one, even the prim little lady plant, somehow bombarding him with its presence.

"You know," Brid said, walking slowly down the aisle, oblivious now of puddles, intent only upon the absorbing and motley collection. "I feel they're watching *us*. I mean look at that one and that one and over there."

Brid was quite right. Every leaf and flowerhead was turning in their direction, stalks were bending, floppy petals were opening wide. A pincushion affair in electric blue was screwing itself up and then relaxing again. A creeper was hurriedly untying its own tendrils. Even a rather superior, stiffnecked plant, regally enthroned in a red plastic pot, was surreptitiously inclining its flower. Brid and Alex watched entranced.

"Yes," boomed the Molk proudly, "one can interpret every gesture when one's familiar with them. But you know it's an awfully good sign that they're noticing you—and that you're noticing them noticing. I mean—they've never made any headway, even with the people who could see us, before. Yes, it's a very good sign indeed." He gazed, impressed, first at his collection and then at the twins. The Molk was suddenly looking solemnly excited.

Brid began to feel a little excited too, inside. Alex just stood and stroked their Ignet Seed affectionately.

The Molk seemed to ponder for a moment.

"And this brings me back to where we were—that is, where we were going to, what I really intended you to see and to know. It is the last thing in our programme. It is in fact the very threshold of our way home. Now that you hold your Ignet Seed, it's time you were shown our most important thing—an Olbaboth."

"An Olbaboth!" exclaimed Brid with awe.

"Here in Kew? For us to see?" asked Alex. They remembered Harragong's words: "With your eyebrows you feel . . . and know in Olbaboth the pulse and centre of all Maboria beat."

"Here in Kew," the Molk nodded solemnly. "For you to see. It's been hard to grow. Very hard. Only Piperada, our Mistress of the Growing Room, has had the patience to coax one into life. And in growing for us a real Olbaboth she has managed, at last, perhaps, to grow us a way home."

The twins waited.

"By Olbaboth we may get back to our Maboria. It's our best loved plant, our most precious flower." The Molk shook his head.

"But nothing is simple, nothing can be straightforward, either here or in Maboria." He scratched at an ear. "You see, although it grows, and Piperada grows it rather well, we—none of us—can persuade the flower to open. We sound the Winehorn loud in Kew, but Olbaboth won't listen. We're afraid that here, and in your time, an Olbaboth will never open for us Maborians. Even an Ignet Seed can't help *us*. The way to Maboria, for my people, is a return to what we've always known. But for you Alex, for you Brid, Maboria *would* be a new beginning, and here in Kew you stand in your own time. So it occurred to Uta, the Ludaz thought, we all hoped, that for you and for your Ignet Seed, our Olbaboth might open, and with it our way home."

He stopped speaking and all was very still. The

great Molk, huge and lofty in his red and golden feathers, looked down gravely at the twins. . . .

"And we are to see the Olbaboth?" Alex asked eventually. "May we see it now?"

"You may. You can see the Olbaboth now—if you will."

"And will it—do we just have to show it our Ignet Seed?" Brid asked uncertainly.

"That's just what we ask you to do. That may persuade it to open. You see, your Ignet Seed, well in a way, it could be both a talisman and guide. It'll be the easiest thing in the world and the most difficult thing in the world. You will lose and you will win. But in you lies the hope of all Maboria."

For a moment he gazed out above their heads and it seemed to Brid and Alex that his mind was a thousand years away.

And then the stillness was broken by a tremendous, silent pandemonium that had broken out all round them. Petals were lifting to the roof, stamens were spreading, leaves flapped and then four times all stems were lowered, four times they stretched again. Voiceless cheers, which the twins could see but did not hear, waved out and out from the collection of the Molk.

Startled, the Molk looked down at his cheering friends.

"Well, well, well, you *are* all stirred up. But I do so agree with all of you. This is a day of days." He lifted up a hand for stillness. "Piperada's told 'em of course," he went on, turning with warmth back to the twins. "For you see *they've* never known Maboria—but that's where they really want to grow."

And us, Brid was thinking to herself, we want to open the way not only because it will help the Maborians, whom we like very much indeed, and want to help, but because we too want to see Maboria properly. But would their Ignet Seed really open an Olbaboth?

She felt for Alex's free hand and found that it was shaking. He wasn't sure, once again, whether it was from fear or from excitement. But his other hand held fast their Ignet Seed and it was a very comforting thing to hold.

CHAPTER TWELVE

It was Piperada, Mistress of the Growing Room, who was taking them to the inmost hall where grew the unopened sleeping Olbaboth. They must wait there for the exiled Maborians to gather. The Molk had said that all the expedition must be there, every single member must be present with the one exception of—himself.

"For I can never be with you—there with Olbaboth," he had said, shaking his head very firmly and very sadly. "All I can do is to summon the others—and wait to hear that what is about to happen has now taken place."

Then they had seen him go off in the other direction, splashing through the puddles in his gumboots, walking slowly among the waving, bowing, exuberant plants of his collection, a tall and stolid but strangely solitary figure.

Piperada was very tiny and her hair was very fair

and piled up high on top of her head. Her feathers were of softest blue tinged with palest pink and she kept moving them about herself, rearranging them, making them point in a different way, leaving gaps and filling spaces in. It was difficult to see exactly how it was done. As she followed her, Brid watched Piperada in fascination. And in spite of all the heat and steam, the little Maborien seemed to stay gloriously cool.

She led them through swing doors—and they had come into a glowing golden-green and twilight place. Before them was another pool, yet unlike Harragong's circular bath, this one was square and walled and as high as their waists and the strange water within was empty, silent and absolutely motionless. The hall itself was high, its walls and roof in glass, grown over by enormous leaves, creepers that grew everywhere.

Quietly Piperada moved to the edge of the pool.

"Come," she said, beckoning. "Come, and you must try and see."

Expectantly they joined her at the water's edge. Only then, when they noticed Piperada's tiny hands clutching the parapet, did they realize how tense and anxious she was. Only with an effort could her voice stay calm. "See," she whispered, so very patiently, "Olbaboth is here, see in the very centre. There is our Olbaboth."

But Alex and Brid did not look out over the water immediately. Not yet. Slowly and long they looked at each other. Instinct, sharpened by all the day's experiences, told them that this was to be their greatest test yet. Before they could hope to open Olbaboth, Olbaboth must first be seen.

And then they looked and the pool was golden-green and glowing and without a ripple and was filled with emptiness.

Piperada was pointing silently over their reflections, over the vague distorted shapes of reflected plants and creepers, pointing to the very heart and vacant centre of the pool.

Brid and Alex half closed their eyes, knowing that it was not a question of just looking for Olbaboth, that they must let the Olbaboth see that Brid and Alex were here.

Little by little it happened. Almost, they understood rather than saw that the golden glow all round them came not only from the sunshine filtering through the window net of creeper leaves, but that it was rising, rising like haze or steam from the very surface of the pool itself. The smooth surface was broken in one small place. An eight-pointed star of leaves seemed to spread as though etched in glass. And then—transparent leaves—they burst aflame, were momentarily there and brilliant. More and more leaves, caught in their own light, were like some dazzling mirage, tier upon tier of stars flickering and gleaming.

Alex, Brid, both held their breath.

In the centre of the stars, a spark of light revealed a single tiny bud, closed tight and smaller than Brid's fist. A strange shimmering tree, still vague and indistinct—but there.

A long sigh escaped Piperada. Her hands relaxed, she smiled. Brid saw tears of relief in her eyes. They trickled helplessly down the Maborien's cheeks.

"OH—I was so worried—so afraid—that you would not be able to see. But I should not have been.

There was no need." Happily she smiled from them and back towards the glimmering tree.

"This is a true and living Olbaboth, the only one to grow outside Maboria. Already it is very beautiful, but still it only sleeps." Wistfully Piperada stared out across the stillness of the pool. "In far Maboria, upon the lakes of Grey and Green, and when the Winehorn sounds, then will an Olbaboth flower. That is a day for happiness. We love, above all else, to look upon the opened flower, to see the shimmer on the golden petals, to feel as if the circle of our time holds still. For Olbaboth is not the hoping for, nor yet the memory of what things were—it is the Now. And happiness can only truly happen—now." She paused, her eyes shining, and then suddenly she looked at the twins and her eyes were sad. "We may all enjoy that happiness—except the Molk himself. He alone must never look upon an Olbaboth."

"But why?" asked Alex wonderingly. "Why not?"

"Because," Piperada almost whispered, "he is the Molk and upon him the endless circle of Maborian time depends. Indeed our circle IS his memory. Should that memory be drained, then our ring would break and all Maboria be flung into the Gulf. So Olbaboth is perilous indeed for him, for if he looks upon its face and sees the Now, he might forget our future and fail to foresee our past. With Now his memory might be erased and our ring of time be snapped. So he, the greatest out of Maberdy, may never see what we Maborians love the best of all."

For a long while they all remained silent. Silence was complete except for a distant drip. Tap-tap. Tap-tap.

Alex and Brid just stood, simply looking at this tree of Olbaboth. It had appeared to them, but would it also open its flower for them? And what would it be like? Would the flower be another gateway and another bridge—a bridge that could safely span the Gulf of Time?

Absorbed in their thoughts, they did not notice the first quiet Maborian enter softly in, nor see them follow one by one, and were surprised at last to look round and see so many there. Maborians, excited and expectant, were coming in, in twos and threes continuously now, walking gently, greeting Piperada and themselves, gazing at Olbaboth, gazing up rather fondly or with a quiet concern. The great glass hall, so eerie and so silent previously, began to fill with hushed and eager voices. Maborians were crowded round the edge of the pool—Brid was beginning to wonder if there was going to be room enough for everyone.

Shyly, unobtrusively, a slight smile, a wave to someone in the crowd and Thobrusk had joined them. He smiled at the twins and nodded his head in approval.

"The wine looks well in the bottle," he assured them, glancing towards the Olbaboth. He shook his dusty-coloured feathers and curled his long body into a sort of sitting position on the low wall that surrounded the pool. Just then the crowd around them thinned and Brid caught a glimpse of rabbit-white hair—it was the Ludaz with Uta close behind.

"Ah my friends," his thick voice greeted them. "Vun of the great things about our dear Molkeza is that no matter how important the occasion, she is alvays late. Und the more important it is—the later vill she be. So there is alvays the time for the quick tea cup. You haf both a great deal in front of you. You vill need a great deal inside of you to think about it. Our good friend Thobrusk here alvays insists that to drink is to think und as I am the Think Man, it follows that I must do a great deal of drinking. Now tell me Brid, is it the milk first, last or don't know, und is the sugar vun lump or none lump?"

He had a glorious tray. It was very, very large and, in spite of his remarks about drink, the teapot and the cups took up only a small part of its surface. Here was a dish of fresh and green living cakes, all growing in a snow-white soil; there were toasted brown bulbs and a pile of golden berries in a bowl, sweet scarlet beans and frosted silver leaves piled high upon a plate.

"Is it really tea?" Brid asked.

With great care the Ludaz had set his tray down beside Thobrusk. His great green eyes swivelled right round to inspect her. Then they swivelled back to his tray.

"Er—milk first and two lumps, please, Ludaz," she said hastily.

"My dear Bridder," and the hands spread wide in mock horror. "Is it really tea? That is an imputation of profound dreadfullity. There is nothing more real, either in your country or mine, than tea ven it is brewed to the splendour. Alvays I brew the Maborian tea. Nobody's tea reaches so far. Ven you drink my tea then you feel it go to your furthest extremities. Ludaz's tea is tea to the toes, tea to the furthest tip of the longest hair—an experience for the finger's end."

"Ludaz!" Uta was regarding him with a steely gleam in her eye. "You say it is the quick cup of tea—yet I can see even the Molkeza arriving before the quickness of my cup. No milk. No sugar. Thank you."

Tea was the last thing Alex wanted at the moment. If only everyone would come and they could concentrate on Olbaboth! He felt strangely exultant now. The Ignet Seed was stretching in his palm and folding down, trying to get comfortable again. However, he took his cup—one lump and milk second—as politely as he could.

Thobrusk was also drinking, looking down at the twins between sips.

"Let the time come. Let the time come and whatever happens remember that we are with you more than you can guess." He nodded thoughtfully and went on. "You understand what we say, not because you understand what we are—you do not know—and not because you understand our language: to you our language sounds like your own. But we are really below words, Brid. We are nearer to meaning, Alex. That is why your tea and ours seems so much the same. What you drink at four o'clock means what we drink at three. It is the meaning that we share. . . . Thank you Ludaz. I will lick a leaf, I think."

"Do not let him alarm you, my friends," the Ludaz assured them, neatly helping himself to a handful of golden berries from the tray and eating as he stood. "You vill do vot you can and you vill come to understand. Meanvile—another cup of tea?"

Brid and Alex accepted gratefully. It was becoming hotter and hotter and the golden twilight was oddly oppressive. Several trays were being passed round now and most of the Maborians were drinking, quickly and informally. Excitement was in the air, but it was a suppressed excitement, an excitement kept respectfully below the surface. Piperada, who had refused tea, was busy ushering yet more Maborians into the hall and directing them to the least crowded places. She still managed to look cool, her feathers drawn back from her arms and shoulders, so that Brid noticed her twisted silver bracelets that tinkled as she moved; and as she directed, she waved her hands about and there was the glitter of tiny rings on tiny fingers.

Suddenly Corbrey was standing beside them, sleek in his raven feathers, a little out of breath and evidently in a hurry.

"Oh excuse me, sir. Madam Brid, excuse me. There is so much time that we may lose the things we have to do in it. The Molkeza will be here, but before she comes, there is something I must give to you, something that the Molk remembers you may need."

"Has he—has he remembered whether Olbaboth does open or not?" Alex asked, feeling almost—well—tantalized.

"Yes and no," Corbrey replied with a smile that showed he understood how Alex felt. "It is not quite so plain as that. The memory of our Molk is like the spokes of some great wheel. The spokes are just enough to support our turn of time, but they are not encrusted with the details of each day. In a sense, we Maborians are ourselves those details, while you, if I may say so, are something more special still in relation to our circle." And Corbrey managed, in spite of the crush, to bow deeply towards them both.

"However, the Molk does know that our Olbaboth, when open, will need this."

He hurriedly produced from among his feathers a small bundle of dampish green moss, which he placed carefully in Brid's hands. "You will remember that you tried to plant a Candletree this morning, before we realized the strength of your time? Well, you see, here is another to replace that which disappeared."

Eagerly Brid and Alex inspected the bundle. They could just make out, entwined among the velvety fibres, the twisting tiny roots, and there was the little trunk, so thin and less than five inches long.

But Corbrey was saying something else. "You must give it to Olbaboth. Maybe this Candletree will grow for you in Olbaboth!" And with these words Corbrey vanished back into the crowd before they could even thank him, let alone ask any questions.

And at that moment a sudden hush fell on the packed assembly. Trays and cups had disappeared. The crowd had now squeezed itself into rows standing all attention, necks craning, heads all turned towards the doors. Instinctively, Brid and Alex stiffened.

A cry went up. "The Molkeza! The Molkeza!"

Kovor and Corbrey were holding open the double doors. There was a whispering rustle of feathers—feathers that swept down from the Molkeza's waist to form a train along the floor, feathers that swept upwards behind her head to make a tall and waving crown, a yard of feathers high, shuddering and lustrous in vivid greens and blue.

The Molkeza looked straight in their direction.

"Coooeeeeee!" she called.

The Molkeza of all Maboria had arrived.

"Cooee," Alex said shyly in return, so softly that she hardly could have heard. But then she had ears on the sides of her head. He knew she heard.

"We are here, Madam," came Thobrusk's voice across the pool. "All who must be present are here and waiting, and he who must not come, he walks alone beneath the trees of Kew."

The Molkeza nodded and her tall crown flashed and nodded too. She came towards them round the pool and the lined Maborians drew back to let her by. She arrived, she turned round, she announced: "This is my real birthday. We can begin!"

Behind them now many of the others crowded forward to get closer to the pool, with eyes sparkling and faces waiting. Brid, the little Candletree still in her hand, was pressed closer to her brother. She could see the Ludaz, poised on the wall, sucking in his cheeks in anticipation, Thobrusk absorbed and patient, Uta frowning with concentration.

In the centre of the still water, there and motionless, was the transparent, almost invisible, Olbaboth.

Brid looked first at Olbaboth and then she watched her brother. He seemed quite confident. She too now felt quite steady and even found herself studying the details of the crowd: Maborians myriad and multi-coloured, some tightly clothed from head to painted toe, befeathered to the ears like owls; others with feathers scattered thinly on brown skins, speckled and sunwashed, some with only tiny feathers at their waists and feet.

"They're going to do it," a voice quavered suddenly from the back of the crowd. And then a great

whispering arose like a wind—Maborian whispering that came and returned like the waves of the sea.

Alex deliberately and slowly raised his arm.

He could feel the Ignet Seed burrowing round in his hand. But what if it doesn't want to be shown? he wondered. Should we have asked it? What can we do if it doesn't? He felt a sudden panic crawl over him.

He felt Brid take a deep breath beside him.

Alex unclenched his fingers. The Ignet Seed lay exposed on his outstretched palm.

They watched. The whole assembly were watching.

The Ignet Seed shuddered. To their delight—to Alex's enormous relief—it burst upward like a big red wig on a stalk, a scarlet furry parachute opening above the pool. A huge and new beginning, it hovered commandingly above the Olbaboth. . . .

And the Olbaboth still shimmered.

All watched. All waited.

The Ignet Seed poised—quivering.

Yet the Olbaboth remained unopened. The single tiny bud remained closed tight—unmoved.

There was a waiting in time. And then in his disappointment, in his bottomless disappointment, Alex knew only that the Ignet Seed was collapsing, that it was refolding, returning to him. Olbaboth was unaltered, yet the Seed shrank, it furled, it lowered itself down into his hand.

Brid stood stock still. Alex could not move. In spite of the sticky, clammy heat their bodies seemed to freeze. Though there were watching, patient Maborians all about them, they felt so awesomely alone. Nothing moved, nothing changed, nothing sounded now but the final rustle of the closing, folding seed.

Was nothing else to happen?

Perhaps the glow within the hall was not so strong—it had returned to its original twilight. The pool was golden-green, without a ripple. The pressing, crowded faces all about them did not move, no eyelid flickered, no lips parted into word or smile. Now there were only endless rows of individual features, pointed ears and turned-up noses, oval eyes and slender eyebrows, but all composed into the one and same unfathomable expression, blank and drained and clean of all emotion; faces that could neither ask for help nor give it to them now. There was Harragong, so beautiful, yet cold, unrecognizable in stillness; the Ludaz without warmth and his expansiveness—now almost grotesque; and Corbrey's nobility had become so perfect as to have no meaning. Thobrusk's face retained its wisdom, but now it was a wisdom beyond all reach, it seemed, forever. They were a row of masks carved in some once solid stone, opaque, carved sharply, but now melting away. Edges were blurring, softening before their eyes. Harragong was fading. Piperada was a shadow. Uta was indistinct. Corbrey and Kovor were crumbling. Ludaz had dissolved into air. Finally Thobrusk was a single standing pillar . . . which blew away. . . .

"We're all alone" Brid said to Alex in an odd little voice, "and the pool—it's empty." She was frightened. Alex, in a distant sort of way, knew she was frightened.

"Olbaboth's gone," he said vacantly. "They've all

gone." He felt bewildered, not certain as to whether he had just woken up from sort of sleep, or had fallen asleep from some kind of waking. Somewhere, so far away, there was a fading sigh, and the echo of a bark as if from the far side of a hill.

The greenhouse was still here, vague in the twilight. The creepers still grew and covered the walls and roof; at the far end the double doors were still closed; the pool with its water walled and blank stretched before them.

"We've failed," Alex said flatly. "We've simply failed. And now they've gone. No—I don't think they went back to Maboria—it wouldn't have happened like that. And they couldn't—the Olbaboth didn't open. It just went. We know we didn't open it. It wouldn't open."

He stood there blinking in the green half-light.

"It just wouldn't open," Brid repeated, wondering now what she meant by these words. It was as if she was almost forgetting. As if it was not possible any more to remember.

And Alex felt tired, desperately tired. Why, he wondered wearily, did these Maborians so often lead to nowhere? Perhaps it *was* better to look away, not to ask too many questions. One should—one should go away and look in another direction.

People said, Brid remembered, that the Maborians were just a legend, just a story. People said that they were not really there.

"Alex," Brid asked doubtfully, "Alex, what do you think we should do now?"

"What can we do, Brid?" Alex asked drearily.

"Well we can't just stand here."

"Shall we go home then? We'd better go home, I

think. Home to Uncle Fred." And Alex felt the tiredness begin to lift a little. He began to feel all sensible. "We're probably late as it is."

She nodded her head. Dear Uncle Fred, always so vague that he never knew where they were, but always so pleased to see them back. Yes, they should do that, they should go home. It was the most sensible thing to do.

And yet . . . they neither of them moved. They just waited in silence, and gazed at the emptiness all around them, at the empty, ordinary twilit greenhouse. They stared down at the Ignet Seed folded quietly and comfortably into Alex's palm, and at the Candletree, tiny and white, stretched across Brid's open hand.

Their two Maborian plants—there were all they had.

CHAPTER THIRTEEN

Brid and Alex, holding the precious plants, stood side by side before the strange, now empty pool. Once they had seen an Olbaboth that had grown in splendour there, and now they waited patiently once more, no longer expecting visions of a magnificent golden flower, a triumphal open gateway or a leaping, growing bridge. They just looked down into the blankness of that water—they would see simply what would be there to see.

They leant over the brick parapet. The pool was far deeper than they had imagined. The golden greenness sank down and down to the bottomless, colourless murk.

Deep, deep down a single pinprick of gold pierced the gloom, a pinprick gradually growing larger and stronger as it rose up steadily and slowly towards the surface.

"A bubble—" murmured Alex. "Pouff! It's burst!" He felt his fringe rise suddenly from his forehead and then fall again.

"Here comes another—there, it's gone! And another—look more and more—Alex, it's like—it's like the aerator in Uncle Fred's aquarium."

"Only much bigger," Alex added. Brid's hair was streaming away up from her ears like a splendid banner, held by a soft but continuous upward draught of wind.

It blew gently but always up from the depths of the pool as steam rises from a pan, and brought with it wisps of torn cloud that floated and hung and rolled back off the water. And now they could begin to make out a distant moaning, a quiet, sad and haunting sound, quieter far than they had heard at the Gate when Brid had balanced on that edge, yet so much louder than the tiny wind in Corbrey's lantern cages.

"A wind of Time," whispered Alex. "Brid, it must be coming up from the Gulf itself—perhaps this pool actually reaches into the Gulf of Time. It seems deep enough—it's like a well that sinks on and on for ever."

"Like the memory of the Molk," said Brid suddenly.

Alex looked at her and nodded. "I know what you mean, Brid—so that he can just go on lowering and lowering his bucket. I saw it a bit like that too."

The wind was blowing freshly on their faces now

and the little wisps of cloud, released from each breaking bubble like pale shreds of smoke, danced high to the roof of the great glasshouse. There they hung, a white majestic tent of obliterating mist, casting a strange and chalky brightness through the half-glow of the golden twilight.

Brid sniffed tentatively at the wind. "It smells more like morning," she said quietly, "early morning."

The pale chalky light reached out to the water below, but the surface was now shiny and undisturbed. A wind still blew, yet the bubbles were no longer bursting. "Yet they're still there," Alex whispered. "Look—they've spread right across the pool."

Yet now the pool seemed shallow, the water had become so brilliantly clear, and they could see the clustered bubbles as a bed of gleaming stones cutting off the depths. They watched, waiting for them to rise again.

"Brid—they can't be bubbles. Surely that's the bottom of the pool? They must be pebbles—and rocks. Look, they're not even all the same shape, and that's sand."

There was weed growing too, brown-fingered hands of weed delicately floating out to feel the water-worn rocks, the veins of white and buff. Alex, practically lying now across the parapet, dipped a cautious finger in and tasted thoughtfully.

"Salt?" Brid asked softly. Slowly Alex nodded. At the same moment there came a cry carried on the wind, the full, clear repeating call of a seagull. The cry trailed away and now they heard a steady rhythmic boom, boom, boom—the unmistakable boom, boom, boom of waves beating on a beach.

"The sea!" cried Brid in wonder. "Oh Alex—we're here—it's our rock pool!" And then they were laughing into their own reflected sunburnt faces, lying on that shelf of rock beside their pool, with the warm sun drying the water from their backs. They were Alex and Brid watching the side-step motion of the little crab across the hazards of cleft and crevice and exposed dry seaweed. They were Alex and Brid watching the great gull hovering in the air above them, a huge fellow, turning so slowly that it might almost be the world moving instead, while the gull himself hung still.

They lay there, savouring the presence of this moment, as they had savoured those other moments only a year ago. They experienced Now. And they were Alex and Brid gazing down into the face of the single magnificent flower, its petals flared back in a wide and blazing circle about a golden shining centre.

This was the flower of Olbaboth and it was open here.

Yet still it was their rock pool: its water held within the circle of the rocks, a golden disc that was the sun reflected, floating in the centre.

"Of course—" Alex thought aloud, rolling over and stretching himself out on the rock, "it had to be like this, Brid. Olbaboth could only be our own Now."

The little crab was squeezing itself awkwardly into a crack between two rocks.

"In our time, yes," Brid replied. "I think in our time we can only see it open in our own way—as we are." She watched the little crab reappear and scuttle off behind a further rock. Alex sat up unhurriedly and began to stroke the Ignet Seed. He stroked it firmly, because that was the way it liked being stroked.

"The Candletree, Brid—have you got it?"

"It's here." She showed it to him, extricating the little tree from the remnants of its covering moss. Then, edging carefully forwards, Brid held the frail stringlike plant out over the water of the pool.

"Shall I? Corbrey said we must give it to the Olbaboth. Should we put it in?"

Alex frowned slightly. "I suppose so. That must be what was meant, because this *is* Olbaboth. But . . . the Candletree looks so small."

"And the water's salt," Brid pointed out worriedly. She looked anxiously down into the pool.

Alex frowned again. "But we know the Candletree's no ordinary tree, Brid. And besides, it does seem right to make the whole history of Maboria grow out of the Now. Past, present and future are all Now at one point. Even our Now has got to be a part of their Maboria if we are going to help them home."

Solemnly Brid released the Candletree and with the faintest splash it fell into the water. There it floated, the thin trunk glistening, and now it was arching itself up and stretching out its roots in extended bliss.

"It seems to like the salt," said Brid. "Look, *look* Alex, it's—it's even beginning to grow."

The Candletree was indeed growing. Not instantly this time, but steadily and certainly. Its roots—those tiny spindly little strands—were swelling and strengthening, twisting and lengthening. Before long they were covering half the pool in wide sweeping semicircles. And already the slender trunk was becoming a stark white tree, reaching up, way up above the level of their heads.

Here, at their noses, were merely the roots of the Candletree; roots already lumping themselves out of the water, a twining mesh of fingers knotting and curling, forming little ledges, then dividing and branching out again; shelving, shaping, changing—still young and white and smooth—yet becoming unmistakable.

"Well" said Brid with some awe, "so that's how Uta gets the Root. The Root is the root of the Candletree."

As suddenly as it had started the little Candletree, now many times larger, had stopped growing. They inspected it carefully. They stood knee-deep in the pool water. Alex handed Brid the Ignet Seed so that he could climb up on to the roots. The tiers of keyboards had appeared—they were smaller, but they were here. There was only one difference. There were no long rows of buttons in between. There was only one single button, alone and in the centre—a button carved with two faces.

Theirs!

Brid climbed up alongside with Alex's help. They looked at the button, at the keys and at each other.

"Should we—shall we press it now?" Brid asked.

Alex nodded. It seemed obvious. Very gingerly they pressed their delicate button and their fingers were drawn upwards, were drawn over the narrow keys, softly, certainly, intensely: they touched.

They did not hear anything. They knew only that

their Root was playing as they knew that they existed. It played in their heads. Here they felt and saw and breathed—they were Brid and Alex running knee-deep—waist-deep—through red and waving flowers and tall green grasses. Stalks were brushing against their bare legs and they were running faster and faster.

Yet still their fingers were touching their keyboard. Still they were aware of twisting, twining roots, and the pool about their feet.

They were standing stock still in the centre of the vast field of waving poppies. Before them, it was a long way away, at the very distant end of the field . . . they felt a rising edge of excitement . . . there was the wide, the shining Inmost Lake of Grey and Green spreading outwards—and springing up from the centre of its surface, a great fountain of transparent leaves that flung themselves out in eightfold clusters and climbed to the height of a tremendous tree.

. . . And they heard a shouting, a shouting far away, like a cheer, like praise.

"Olbaboth. Olbaboth."

There was no need to do any more running. They were standing on the very edge of the Inmost Lake and on the other side of that green-tinged silver mirror, there were Maborians, a waiting crowd along the shore, but they were far away.

A bird of blue and sepia flew slowly over them on long and slender wings and they watched its twice-as-long reflection cross the surface of the Lake. They saw their own reflections, green and tall, look out and back and up at them. Alex lifted up his hand and a high green Alex stretched a hand across the water in return. Brid stepped down into the Lake, holding up the Ignet Seed and hitching her skirt, but the water hardly reached her knees. There were no ripples! Neither the water, nor their reflections, were disturbed.

"Alex," she whispered. "It's not wet."

He joined her. He nodded. It was like floating on one's knees above a looking glass. Yet whatever it was, they could walk through it, and their feet were on moss and they were dry.

Now there was no calling, and the mirror through which they waded was silent. They held hands and the reaching reflections before them held hands too. Their images reached across the Lake, reached out towards the Olbaboth. But behind them like shadows, their own figures were still standing before the Root. Still their fingers lay across the keys.

"We're everywhere, Brid," Alex breathed and he could not say any more.

The mirror was not cold to wade through. It was not warm. It was so like themselves that it was hardly there. Apart from the great and rising Olbaboth, it was empty. They walked and walked, out towards, out under the upflung, bounding, climbing tree that is neither gnarled nor old, for it is never touched by Time. The branches that bear the leaves are red and smooth and spiked like some gigantic rose. The leaves themselves spread out like elegant hands, hands that trail down to points and yet are broad and kind; and at the top, rising in fullness, glowing and golden, grows the bud that will become the flower.

Harragong had said—"You have to climb the tree."

Upward and upward.

Brid tried to concentrate on climbing. High as the stem rose, it proved so simple to go up. Her hands and feet reached from spike to spike, each spike curved upward to make a foothold, a handhold, and Alex climbed with her. They hardly seemed to recognize each other. They just climbed.

Upward and upward.

Olbaboth swayed slowly in the breeze.

They clung.

"Look, Alex, look," Brid cried. She could not help herself.

They hung at the centre of a world. Back and back below stretched green waters and wide meadowland, meadows climbing towards distant hillsides, filled with dancing blossom and arching trees, meadows that were cities, cities that grew and were alive, Maberdy in Maboria, waiting to be explored. Patches and splashes of colour interweaved into the distance—orange, green and silver—dark blues and umber. Water fell and rainbows plunged and pathways raced outward, newly vanishing through and pointing still further beyond. The eye went feasting.

The Molk's world! Alex thought. Here he ruled and here the Molkeza rode and here all things tasted and music was made. Here Thobrusk had made deep wine and here the Ludaz thought. Here, before they had gone away to Kew, Kovor had grown his harp and sung; here Corbrey dwelled. This was what both he and they were waiting for.

"Come on, Brid."

They climbed.

Upward and upward.

The great leaves hung about their ears like translucent banners, dazzling their eyes with reflected light. Two more pulls and at last they were at the top, clinging to the final spikes, their feet level with the ripening golden bud.

It was then that they heard it.

Boi—rmmmmmm m m m m. Boi—rmmmmmm m m m m.

The Winehorn of Maboria was sounding and sending its rich and mellow rolling notes echoing through their heads.

Boi—rmmmmmm m m m m.

And the golden bud responded. The golden bud was stirring, breaking open, the petals quivering until they burst into a radiant sun.

The face of Olbaboth stared out at them from all the lengths of Time, and looked out across all places, grew out of all reflection. When closed, the Olbaboth held everything. Open—all things could enter in, all things flowed out from it.

Brid and Alex gazed. And they also heard. The flower spoke in their ears, spoke without words. It called unwords in their heads, meanings that they understood though their tongues could not have said them. And then those meanings curled out from the Olbaboth like smoke into their minds, curled into a memory that they could never untie. This moment, thought Brid. Yes, this moment, thought Alex.

Yet as they gazed, as they clung, a dizzy height above the Lakes of Grey and Green, half lost in the great blossom, their figures behind them still stood before the Root, watching them as if a million miles away.

Now the Ignet Seed was struggling in Brid's fist.

She opened her fingers to give it more room but it burst outward and splendid from her hand, a huge and furry parachute, it swung over the open flower. The new beginning, their new beginning, hung above the open mouth of all Maborian Now, and Olbaboth opened more, opened its green throat and the Seed went floating down, victoriously down, and the blossom brightened . . .

But the sweep of the parachute caught Brid off her balance. Alex saw her sway and then she was toppled, drawn, vanished, swallowed by the mighty centre of all Maboria. She had fallen forward, helpless, downward, inward, through the maw and timeless centre of the Olbaboth.

He yelled.

All Alex screamed and grabbed for his sister and his hands, her hands, lifted off the manuals of the Root, lifted off—disconnected.

The playing ceased.

He was back in front of the tiers of keys and buttons and the twisting, rising, climbing branches of the Root.

And he was alone.

CHAPTER FOURTEEN

Alex blinked. For a frozen moment he could do nothing, think of nothing, know nothing—except that his sister had vanished, had disappeared down an Olbaboth, falling, falling, and he was—where?

He was back at the Root, surrounded by the twisting Candletree. There were the keys running round in semicircles and the buttons, each carved with a head—the Molkeza's the most prominent of them all.

But where was the Inmost Lake of Grey and Green? He was no longer clinging to the swaying Olbaboth. Olbaboth had taken his sister and had not taken him at all, while he was back at the keyboard of their Root—alone.

Buttons?

He looked up and round. This was not their rock pool. It was not their rock pool at all. This was the Maborian Root Room that he had come back to. He rushed to the entrance.

There was the Kew Lake in the late afternoon, the lines of green trees in the yellow sunlight, the ducks lazily navigating the smooth water, a black swan like an ocean liner forcefully forging on towards some distant shore.

At his feet, moored to the doorway, was the curious and fragile boat shaped like a leaf. Seated cross-legged in the middle of it was Uta.

"Uta!" Alex cried.

Uta looked up, not with surprise but with a certain smile.

"Ah—wonderful," she said. "You have done what I have expected. You have come back. That is even more impressive than disappearing from the middle of us all in the first place."

"But Uta, Uta—it's Brid."

Uta nodded sympathetically. "I know. Come into the boat. We must first join the others. It is the only way. A great many things are going to happen while we do not expect them. Trust Uta."

With a firm hand she helped Alex into the boat

and then swiftly pushed off into the Lake. Alex crouched in the stern. He felt reassured by Uta's certainty, though startled at her insistence that Brid and he had done the disappearing. Now he found himself staring hard at the water, at the rushes and the grassy banks, and the distant trees, in case they should all disappear if he looked away. But the trees stayed in their places, the banks remained green, lush and unchanged. No one seemed to be about—except once there was a glimpse of something, someone, moving in the distance, a solitary figure walking among the trees.

Skilfully, Uta directed her boat in among the rushes and edged it against the bank. She jumped out over Alex and then whistled an electrifying double note.

"Hubble," she shouted. "Hubble, Hubble, Hubble."

It was a Kylin, a scarlet Kylin, red as a bus, streaking through the trees towards them, eyes like lighted amber, lower, longer, fleeter, than Afghar. He was saddled with high twin black saddles, harnessed in tandem to his back.

"To arrive in time—we will have to hurry," Uta explained. "To arrive out of time is far too complicated."

Hubble panted, crouching and bubbling before them. Alex swung up behind Uta. The whole Kylin vibrated between his knees. There seemed to be no bridle, no rein, with which to control him. Evidently they were not needed. The red Kylin just had to be told.

"Shift, Hubble."

With a kind of screeching whine Hubble

launched across the Gardens. Alex held on. Everything was all right so long as he held on.

"We must now join the others," Uta explained over her shoulder. "They are waiting by the Palm House. When you went, we watched the Olbaboth not opening." Alex began to protest, but stopped. Anyway Uta was continuing—"Then suddenly it began to grow. How it grew! It grew beyond all our calculations. It filled the water tank—it reached the roof—what were we to do with it? The Molkeza panicked, of course. The Ludaz said we must re-pot it. So now we have floated it on the Pond before the Palm House. There it is splendid. It is still growing. You will see. But still it does not open. NOW Hubble!"

Hubble jumped. A green hedge sailed under them. They dodged neatly between the rose trees. Alex had to lean over as Hubble went round corners. They were up on a terrace . . . there was Harragong's bath-house to the left . . . and now the big Palm House stood above them, like a tethered glass balloon full of trees on a glass platform, and Hubble was careering round to the front.

Every Maborian, every Maborien, surely must be here. And not only that, but every Kylin that had ever come to Kew was here as well. There were dozens of the beasts, some standing neatly saddled in rows (one saddle, two saddles and even three), others sitting on their haunches or even lying down. They were thick and square and shaggy and were mostly in greens and browns and blacks, purring and rumbling, licking at their paws and at each other, scratching contentedly, but all keeping a glaring eye on what was happening, snoffelling and gluffering at each other as if in comment, tails beating. One was lapping up bucketfuls from the Pond.

A sudden shudder of excitement ran through Maborians and beasts alike at the arrival of Hubble. Uta dismounted. Alex followed. Eager hands helped and everyone made way for them. Alex could now see the Pond properly. There it was, a wide stretch of water surrounded by willows and cypresses and some odd plant that he had always thought looked just like giant rhubarb. And there, rising above the Pond's surface, close to the steps that led down into the water, was a great spiked leaping trunk, transparent eightfold leaves held high—the exiled Olbaboth.

But this bud was still closed.

Only the Molk was not there to greet Alex.

Kovor, looking hot and with his yellow feathers all over the place, was still checking that the Olbaboth was safely settled, while Piperada, her glorious hair all tumbled round her shoulders now, was anxiously wiping down the precious leaves. Even Corbrey looked flustered as he was trying, not very successfully, to untangle the harness of the Kylins used to transport the great tree. Harragong was marching up and down giving orders all round. Thobrusk, a glass in his hand and surrounded by swollen skins of wine, was concentrating hard upon the taste of Time. The Ludaz alone appeared to be content and unconcerned. He was simply sitting on the bottom step with his feet dangling in the water.

Perhaps he's fishing, Alex wondered, but no, he couldn't be, for when the Ludaz saw Alex he turned enthusiastically, splashing with his feet in a way that would have frightened any lingering fish.

"Velcome back Alex, my dear friend," the Ludaz cried. "Velcome home. Ah—ve are having a most quiet time at present—but see vot you haf done by not being here—and just imagine therefore vot you can make happen now that you are back again." And he nodded his head admiringly.

"See how healthily it grows, Alex," Piperada added, turning her dazzling smile upon him. "But oh—it is in such a hurry!"

"Your fingers are greener than ours, you see," Kovor grinned, pausing at his task. "And it gave us a job that we nearly didn't manage, did we Corb?"

Before Corbrey could comment, Alex was swept off his feet by the Molkeza embracing him exuberantly on both cheeks. He simply didn't hear what she had to say. He wished Brid was here—if only to syphon off her share of the enthusiasm.

Thobrusk now put down his glass and looked directly at Alex. His eyes smiled.

"Do not fear for Brid," he said quietly. "Olbaboth takes care of its own. It is harder in a way for those left outside. The taste of the wine is now fading. That is the certain sign. Our Olbaboth will be opening. When the bud unfurls then and for that moment the wine's taste will depart. All time will have become one." Quizzically he cocked an eye towards the swaying Olbaboth. "I think," he added, "that the moment will be soon."

"We shall have another emergency if it isn't," Harragong declared with relish.

The Olbaboth continued to grow. Alex could see it grow as he watched—he could see it draw itself up to the sun, could see each glistening leaf broaden, each spike grow longer. The swelling bud grew brighter and now the central branch was bending under its weight, curving in a great arc towards the heads of the waiting crowd below.

Alex stared at the strange tree. It was this very strangeness that seemed to make it so lovingly familiar. He felt he knew every curving spike and every shining star of leaves. Each leaf was colourless and yet reflected colours in his head, and with every passing moment the stains grew deeper.

Suddenly everything inside him made sense. Suddenly he saw what was not happening. Alex ran down the steps and began to shout as loudly as he knew how.

"Brid!" he cried, "Brid!" he called up desperately towards the tree of Olbaboth. "Brid! BRID! BRID!"

His voice echoed across the Pond, across the crowded Maborians, across the Palm House, across all Kew Gardens.

There was a silence—absolute silence. And then, in the middle of the saddled Kylins, the biggest Kylin, a huge and high black beast lifted up its mighty head and bayed:

"WROOO WOOO IOUOO."

For Olbaboth had cracked, the Olbaboth in exile had opened, immense and golden and lovely. The huge petals were stretching out like sails and all who looked upon the flower stood transfixed, alive, wonderfully alert, feeling with the brows of their eyes, their fingers listening to the worlds, to the long repeated wisdom of the pulse of Olbaboth.

"Brid!" shouted Alex again and his voice sounded small. "Brid!" he repeated more determinedly.

And then from the great golden mouth, like a scarlet parachute, like a huge umbrella, vast as vast, emerged the Ignet Seed and clutching at its end was Brid, who came floating down into the crowd.

"Explosion!" cried the Molkeza.

Brid landed smoothly on the grass, still clutching the scarlet Ignet Seed and then—let go!

The Ignet Seed floated upwards and sailed over the Palm House.

"It's away!" called Harragong excitedly.

But Alex had already reached his sister. Maborians who had rushed forward to pick her up stood back respectfully.

"Alex—how did you get here? I heard you calling. No, I just caught hold of the Seed when I fell—it almost seemed to wait for me. And then it led me slowly down and down and down. It wasn't dark at all, it was green, brilliant green—a glowing shiny green, like emeralds. And there were endless gleaming edges in all directions. They flickered and smouldered and—oh Alex, I could see it all so clearly. Everything led everywhere and nowhere in particular. I would like to have gone on floating always." Her voice trailed off and she frowned slightly. A scarcely audible sigh rose up like a breeze from the assembled Maborians.

Brid became aware of Thobrusk's penetrating gaze upon her. She had never seen him look so stern before.

"But the Seed did know which way to go," she continued firmly. "And then I heard you calling,

Alex. We began to go faster and faster and suddenly the green became gold and then I could see blue—and it was sky."

"But where have you come from?" Uta asked precisely, not because she did not know, but because she felt it should be said out loud, so that all could hear.

Brid looked up happily. She realized now to the full what had happened, what they had done, what had happened for all of them.

"From Maboria," she answered clearly. "Alex and I went there through our own Root and the Ignet Seed has led me back through the Olbaboth itself."

"THE WAY BACK," Harragong was simply jigging up and down, "the way back is open!"

"It is open," Thobrusk agreed, and though he spoke gently the most distant Maborian could hear. "Olbaboth is open in a strange land and we who come from far Maboria are glad. Our friends have opened Olbaboth—and they have shown that through the Olbaboth itself is our way home. We need only a new beginning to lead us, and the courage to return. But do not forget—we must never forget that these our friends have made it possible."

Then all at once the surrounding Maborians drew back, and in silence they lifted up their hands towards the twins and then they smiled—a strange mysterious smile, as if they knew everything that Brid and Alex had ever known, and everything that they could look forward to.

But then:

"Mount!" Harragong cried. "Come ON everyone—the Seed is loose. Only the Seed will know the way back through the Olbaboth. To the Hunt! Collect up the Kylins. Everyone gather behind the Palm House, for there the Molk can join us, beyond the sight of Olbaboth. Maborians—we must hunt this new beginning for ourselves."

CHAPTER FIFTEEN

"You know, Brid, you know Alex—" the Molk was saying, "every time you open up the way home through Olbaboth, I marvel at how you've done it."

They were waiting with him now on the terrace above the Rose Garden beyond the Palm House. The scene about them was one of indescribable confusion—a turmoil of excited feathers and panting shaggy fur. Everywhere Maborians were buckling on harnesses to impatient Kylins, helping to saddle those unsaddled, trying to comfort those uncomfortable.

Alex looked up at the Molk and grinned. He'd just had a glorious thought. "But we haven't *done* it exactly—not yet," he said.

The Molk looked down at the twins. And then grinned back.

"Go on then, Alex. Tell me how far you haven't done it yet."

"Well Sir, we've only got this far by remembering through our Root. And like before, we seem to have remembered our future instead of our past. So unless we actually *do* go to Maboria with you, we can't have the future we're now remembering."

Alex gave Brid's hand a triumphant squeeze

while the Molk's grin grew considerably broader.

"You're quite right of course, Alex," he replied. "I might add that you make it all sound a good deal simpler than when the Ludaz explains it. And—" the Molk hesitated, "and do I take it that you *want* to come back with us?"

"Not only want to—going to," Brid declared. She was dancing about madly.

The Molk stood motionless. He just looked hugely pleased.

But although Alex knew that he was quite sure about all this, there was one point . . . "What I don't understand is how Brid, by going down one Olbaboth could come up out of another?"

"That's really quite simple," the Molk assured them. "Olbaboth is the NOW. Wherever you go, whenever you go, whichever of you goes, the Now is always the NOW. The Now Brid feels when she wakes, the Now Alex knows at lunch, the Now Uncle Fred loses when he sleeps—they're all one. I know that sometimes they seem different." He smiled. He was remembering. "The Now you felt at the rock pool seems very big, very important. The Now you have when you're running for one of your trains may seem very small. It's just that you've opened your eyes on one—on the other they're almost closed. In the same way, there may seem to be many Olbaboths in many sizes. Yet they're always the same Olbaboth, no matter where they grow. If you fall down one, then you may come out of another."

"Oh I see," Brid exclaimed. "I see—but then is it the same with the Root? I mean, Alex started playing at one Root and finished up at a different one. Are they really all the same too?"

"Not quite," pondered the Molk. "Perhaps it's easier to think of it this way: as you know, the Roots are memory—in this case your particular memories—and it's not so much that the Roots are the same, it's *you* who remain the same."

Brid had just got her mind nicely wrapped round all this when a piercing whistle cracked her ears.

"Come ON, Umbrij!" the Molkeza called.

They looked up with alarm. So this was Umbrij, Alex thought, remembering the portrait hanging halfway up the long Pagoda stairs. Umbrij was the fiercest Kylin of them all. He was absolutely white, with bright red eyes, and he was charging the Molkeza with a mighty "WOOF", teeth bared and froth bubbling from his jaws.

"Don't get quite so excited, dear," Harragong complained, stepping sharply to one side.

"WRAAGH!"

With an agile leap Harragong was astride his back. Umbrij wore no saddle. She gripped him between a powerful pair of knees. He bucked, he reared, he glared—and had his nose tapped with a silver foot. Harragong might have been fastened on with glue.

"Come on, dearie—up the front."

And they galloped off towards the other side of the Rose Garden where the main Hunt was assembling.

"I thought you might like to ride with me," the Molk suggested. "It'll be perfectly safe. Can't go in for high jinks at my size. Besides, Bastif wouldn't like it. Yes. My Kylin's Bastif—the biggest one.

Has to be. That's right, the black one over there. Here he comes."

Bastif was enormous, glossy, thunderous, black as night, and bounding ponderously towards them. The Molk got an affectionate buffeting and Alex had his face washed with one sponge-like lick.

"No, boy!" said the Molk sternly and before Bastif could start on Brid. And then Brid found herself being lifted up on to the front saddle, safely out of tongue's reach. She grabbed the silken curly mane to steady herself. The Molk heaved himself up behind her and pulled Alex up behind him.

"That's it. Now Bastif—slowly."

Many Maborians were on their Kylins now, lining up behind the Molkeza, and carrying huge pale-coloured nets like lances with banners, as if to capture giant butterflies. Brid admired their handling of their mounts, riding casually, bare-legged and astride, one hand on hip, the other holding high a net, controlling the excited rumbling beasts with jabs from foot or knee.

"I don't hunt seeds myself," the Molk boomed over Brid's head. "Leave that to Harragong. But one does get a splendid view from up here."

This was perfectly true—they were that much higher up than anybody else.

"That's Corbrey isn't it?" Alex asked from behind.

"That's Corbrey," agreed the Molk. "He's up on Minsta. Quietest hound we have. Gallop at thirty miles an hour and you can hardly hear her breathe. Kovor's there as well. On Charko. She's a splendid Kylin—when she's in the mood. Steady Bastif! Whoa boy! He always did like Charko."

Charko was facing towards them; one large and delicate ear held up, one held demurely down. Brid waved to Kovor, who waved back enthusiastically, whereupon Charko, disgusted at her master's divided attention, turned right round disgruntedly to face the other way. However, she had a magnificent tail that curved like a canopy over Kovor's head.

The Molkeza was making an announcement.

"Everybody! This is me. Now, when we first see the Seed I want you all to give tongue. If a thing's worth doing, it's worth doing loudly. PIPERADA! I want to start."

"Pipz's Kylin is the best smeller," the Molk whispered into Brid's ear. "Look, she's bringing it forward now. This is the big moment. Otherwise they won't know which way to go. She rides Buffon. Buffon's got a wonderful nose."

Buffon jingled. He did not carry Pipz for nothing. Not only did she wear bracelets and anklets and rings, but her Kylin did too. His harness was far more elaborate than that of his fellows; it was covered in bells and there were copper bands round his tail and paws, and as he came forward he jigged on all four of them. His nose was wide and the nostrils curled.

Pipz leaned forward and tapped him just between the ears.

Everyone was still. The Kylins stood like statues —except for Buffon.

He sniffed.

"Moww?" he said exploringly.

He sniffed again.

"MOWW!"

And now Piperada could not restrain him. He was away.

"There it BLOWS!" Harragong called.

"This is it," the Molk remarked to himself, letting Bastif get up steam in the rear.

And then like terrible thunder the whole Hunt of High Maboria in Exile swept out between the trees of roses, between the tall green hedges, at full gallop, pell-mell and growling, barking, barking, barking, out into the wilds of Kew.

"Can you see it all?" Alex asked anxiously, leaning out from his saddle. So far they had no view of the Ignet Seed and now even the tail end of the Hunt was rapidly disappearing from sight.

"In a little while," the Molk reassured him, "in a little while we'll see it. The Seed is only playing now."

"But supposing it gets away?"

"The Seed wants to be caught—eventually. But it must believe it's captured. When it is time—Bastif will be there."

Brid had her doubts about that. Bastif was now just ambling, positively *ambling*. He seemed far more concerned with the flowers in the grass than with the Hunt. Well, she supposed, this was a relief after that first mad sprint . . . and then she heard a great beating of paws up behind them. It was the Ludaz astride a somewhat tattered-looking Kylin with a rather tousled head.

"The Seed, she has got avay, my friends. She has dodged down the Rhododendron Dell. But Dagleff is viley. Come on—ve vill head it off for them. Not for nothing is Dagleff the Think Dog," and he cantered madly off under the trees, swaying dangerously.

The Molk was alerted.

"AFTER HIM, BASTIF. They need us—even if only to save the Ludaz. Hold tight. HEIGH YO! BASTIF."

With a great hiss, the mightiest Kylin of Maboria began to move. Brid and Alex might have felt impatient before. Now they just shut their eyes and clung.

It was nearly a minute before Brid dared to open hers. The trees fled by. There was Dagleff in front and harum-scarum Kylin though he seemed to be, he could certainly move. Perhaps the joggling Ludaz was safer than he looked. Perhaps! He seemed to have fallen forward on his hound.

"Duck, Brid," the Molk warned and a bough swished by above their heads.

"Did I not say that it goes?" the Ludaz shouted ahead and he swerved off dangerously and downhill to the left, his arms waving.

Alex opened his eyes. Perhaps he was getting used to it. The Ludaz was right. There, floating temptingly just above the ground, scarlet and twirling, just ahead was the Ignet Seed; and as Dagleff approached, it was away, darting, spinning and climbing.

Bastif let out a great roar, banked sharply and bounded over a flower bed. And then there was a loud barking the other way and up came the whole Hunt straight towards them, nets raised and flying and furious—and Harragong, Harragong way out in front and laughing, Umbrij speeding, speeding madly, growling and foaming. There was the Seed floating, turning calmly up between a clump of rhododendrons.

"Oh it will be caught, it will be caught," gasped Brid.

Harragong swept in. "It's me! It's me!" she shouted.

SWISH!

It dodged her.

The whole Hunt closed in. Bastif reared up hard to avoid a collision. There was Ludaz with Dagleff again, all by himself, streaking through the trees, Ludaz lying headlong, his arms round his Kylin's neck.

But the Ignet Seed had dodged round them all and there was a great turmoil among the rhododendrons while everybody tried to ride out again and then Bastif took his chance to stop the Seed's escape and charged in.

The Ludaz had disappeared from sight.

Brid gritted her teeth. Alex felt a marvellous upsurge of terrible excitement.

"The Molk! The MOLK!" the Molk cried.

And the Seed tried to dart back, but there was Piperada with blue net billowing and half a dozen Maboriens with her, their Kylins yelling; and it went to the side but Corbrey swept silently up on its flank and Kovor on Charko was just behind and Hubble blocked the main path of escape and here was Harragong again and they encircled and Umbrij was on it and Harragong's net was raised—but the Seed found a narrow gap, shot through, and was gone.

There was a startled pause.

"wooooo!" Umbrij wept.

Now utter confusion. Bastif stopped stock still, shaking his great head sadly. Uta had got out her compass to find out where West was. Buffon was trying to sniff. Minsta had shut her eyes and Charko decided that this was the moment for a good shake.

"It's shake the teeth out of my head that you will and why do it when it's wet, which you are not?" Kovor complained.

"Which way, my Buffon?" Pipz was asking anxiously. "Which way?" Buffon was sniffling, was dancing round and round, but nothing came. The Ignet Seed had gone.

The Molkeza took charge. She had already dismounted and was trying to cheer up Umbrij.

"There, there. Now relax everyone. Time for the interval. Let the beasts get their breaths back. There, THERE, Umbrij. He gets so upset. Do make Buffon sit down, Pippa dear. Of course he can't smell anything, he's panting too much—and making me dizzy. Do keep him still. Let everyone get their breath back."

Harragong seemed to have plenty of breath.

"Good-oh," the Molk said. "Down, Bastif. Down boy."

Brid and Alex slid off and it was only then that they realized how sore they were already.

Maborians dismounted—stretched—put their nets down, smoothed, rearranged or just hitched at their feathers.

Kylins collapsed, lay down, sat down or just stood and gasped, with blunt jaws hanging wide. The Molk sat on the grass and settled himself comfortably against the back of the seated Bastif. Alex and Brid sat too.

Afghar suddenly appeared, sidling through the grouped Kylins, grunting and purring, Thobrusk calm and unexcited on a single saddle astride. Without orders it seemed, Afghar mooched up to Bastif and there lay down. Afghar rumbled a greeting. Bastif mumbled back. Thobrusk unwound himself from Afghar's back.

"When the fruit ripens," the Vintner remarked, addressing both the Molk and the twins, "then comes all the tiresome business of the picking and the packing."

The Molk nodded heavily. "How *is* the packing, Thobrusk?"

"Well, it was one thing to bring everything with us when we came. It is going to be quite a different matter to take it all back."

"I feared as much," the Molk said gloomily. "Everything's grown so. And then there are all the new collections. We shall just have to leave some of it behind."

"Perhaps to be appreciated by your Uncle Frederick," Thobrusk suggested, smiling at the twins. But almost immediately he was serious again. "You are yourself our greatest problem, Sir. For you may not look upon the flower of Olbaboth, and yet now we have to ask you to travel down its very throat."

The Molk stared out in front of him. One big hand absentmindedly began to tickle Bastif's snoozing head. Brid glanced up anxiously at the Molk—for an awful moment she imagined him left behind. Well, *she* was not going to Maboria without him, and that meant that nobody could go.

The Molk sighed. "It won't be easy, Thobrusk. I just mustn't notice. You'll have to blindfold me when the time comes. You'll have to block my ears and bind my hands. We shall have to take the risk."

Thobrusk stared at the ground and a flicker of concern passed across his face. Brid remembered how penetrating had been the glistening shining greenness that had been within.

"Someone," the Molk continued, almost apologetically, "I'm afraid someone will have to lead me. I mean—Harri would. But she's got to manage Umbrij." He gave a wry grin. "Harri's the only one who can. Can't leave him behind. Don't think Uncle Fred would appreciate Umbrij."

Brid didn't even smile—but she answered. "Alex and I—we'll take you through, on Bastif. I can remember what it's like, so perhaps I can help you not to notice. And Alex'll manage to handle Bastif."

As if in response, the great dog licked one of Alex's knees.

The Molk bowed his head and squeezed Brid's hand.

"Thank you," he said simply. "Thank you, my dears."

A whistle blew loudly.

"UP EVERYBODY," the Molkeza cried. "UP, UP, UP. We hunt again. Buffon tastes of the wind."

"Duty calls," groaned the Molk, heaving himself to his feet. "Any other problems, Thobrusk?"

"Nothing in particular—a wineskin leaking here and there. They never did fit into anything very conveniently. As a matter of fact I had hoped—I was wondering if Uta might come and help. It's only when they haven't fitted that I realize that they don't. She could save me a great deal of time, I think." And nodding hopefully, the Vintner climbed back on to his Kylin.

The Molk put Brid into Bastif's second saddle this time, and helped Alex climb up into the first. "I can see Alex wants to have a go," he said approvingly. "No, I'm not even coming up behind this time. I think I ought—I suppose I must go and do some packing. Now Bastif—be good!"

"Uruumph!" Bastif said, rather deeply down.

"Hush," everybody else was saying. Buffon smelt the air.

"There it blows AGAIN," Harragong's voice throbbed over them and the whole Hunt, Bastif included, were on the move.

A little shyly, Alex leaned forward and patted Bastif. He really felt a bit impertinent—Bastif was such a very large animal. But in any case, he doubted whether his pat had even penetrated. And yet—the Kylin shuddered under him and they gathered speed quite noticeably.

Brid held on—hard. Bastif was only just behind Umbrij—now Buffon was tearing along beside them, Minsta padded swiftly to their left and the rest of the Hunt was actually behind. Again Harragong unfurled her net, Piperada swung hers high, Corbrey's was aimed forward like a lance. Just ahead of them, and only just ahead, was the flying, gliding Ignet Seed.

Alex had been watching the riders most carefully. Now, more confidently, he reached forward with his foot and plunged it into the curling black and silken mane.

At once Bastif responded. He was pulling ahead. They had left Buffon behind. They were careering along the side of the Lake, ducks and geese were scattering, moorhens fled. Bastif gave tongue:

"WROO WOO IOUOO."

"He obeys," Alex called delightedly. "Wonderful boy!" They narrowly missed a tree but Alex did not care. His feet steered Bastif. He felt, Brid felt, the whole of Kew fly past them; but they were part of it, the race of the Kylins, the ride of the Maborians, the growth of the rising trees, the change of the plants as time beat by. And ahead, ahead the Ignet Seed was turning away from the Lake.

There was a great rumbling roar beside them, Umbrij was beginning to sprint....

"Cooeee—no one goes faster than Harragong even if Bastif has got a new speed with new masters. Heigh Ho, Umbrij! Left—you mongrel—left."

Harragong on Umbrij turned more sharply than they did, with Harragong leaning right out to keep her balance. Bastif came round more slowly, but his stride was still longer. They were neck and neck. There was the Pagoda, far ahead.

"Now let us run it down," the Molkeza exalted. "No Seed has ever beaten me. HEIGH HO, UMBRIJ!"

She lowered her net and Umbrij charged ahead. High up to the right on its mound—Brid caught a glimpse—the Gate that she had opened was closed; but already it was behind her and the Seed was gliding round the high Pagoda itself—round, round to the left again, and Kovor was near them and Corbrey was padding alongside.

Left, left, Bastif pounded on, but where was

Harragong? Where was the Seed? The Hunt was fanning out. Was the scent lost?

But there was the Seed again, just ahead, and there was the long white building on a terrace with the King and Queen over the door—and high over the trees to the right was the flagpole. The revolving red umbrella Seed swerved and Alex steered Bastif in pursuit.

"It will not be long now," came Kovor's voice behind them. "It's ahead beyond the hedge in the Rose Garden that it will stop when we arrive, which will mean it can't get out if we are in the way," and Charko was off in another direction.

"Follow me," came Corbrey's unexpected whisper. "I can take you to the most important position. It is always so important to see."

He rode so upright, so perfectly upon his black saddle with his black harness and his black Kylin. Minsta winked at Bastif and waved a club-like tail.

"How do you all know where it's gone?" Alex called, but Corbrey did not seem to hear, while Bastif certainly seemed to follow.

They had arrived back at the Rose Garden.

Brid observed that the five gaps, which punctuated the high thick hedge surrounding three sides of the Rose Garden, were filled by mounted Maborians with nets upraised. The final side was taken care of by the billowing, rounded glass of the Palm House itself. Admittedly the Palm House had a doorway through its centre and this door was in fact open, but planted in front of it at the top of the steps, planted very firmly and seated on Dagleff was the Ludaz himself.

Before him, turning slowly now like a huge and tasselled scarlet mushroom, revolved the Ignet Seed—an Ignet Seed trying to get through that doorway.

Dagleff stood still, all four paws straddled wide. The Ludaz leaned forward and faced the Seed with a piercing stare over his Kylin's ears, and he spread out both his arms as far as they would reach, his hands flapping at the ends.

"You shall not pass," he declared. "I am far too big to go round."

The Seed spun about. Dagleff snarled. The Seed retreated. Dagleff barked. The Seed backed away down the steps. It was surrounded. It was trapped.

Then Corbrey rode forward on Minsta. And Corbrey spoke, yet not in a whisper, but in a voice as clear as cold spring water on a summer day. All round, along the terrace and along the hedges, between the beds where later on the roses bloomed, the Maborians stayed still.

"Make silence. Make silence for her most illustrious, most indomitable, most implacable, most infallible—"

"That's ME," Harragong cried, riding out into the centre with her net held high.

"Madam—will you challenge this Seed?"

Umbrij sidled half away. Harragong shook back her long black hair, with a half smile upon her face.

"I will." She held out her net.

There was a gigantic silence.

The Molkeza looked at the Seed.

The Seed looked at the Molkeza.

Nobody moved.

("Why doesn't it just fly away?" Alex asked in an undertone.

"Because," said a voice behind Bastif, "that would be the cowardice which it hasn't got, so it won't do it and therefore it must stay, if you hear what I mean.")

The Molkeza never took her eyes off the Ignet Seed for a moment. "I am HARRAGONG," she declared.

The Seed shuddered.

Umbrij crouched.

Brid gasped because the Seed began to grow. It became larger and larger—bigger than a parachute, bigger than a scarlet tree, higher than the Palm House, overshadowing Harragong, overshadowing the whole Rose Garden. Brid wanted to go back and back. She wanted Bastif to turn. The Ignet Seed was getting bigger and bigger, it was blotting out the sun.

The Molkeza did not move. She spoke again. She did not speak more loudly, only a little more slowly, and still her net remained upraised.

"I am still HARRAGONG."

She sat upright in her saddle and Umbrij was not afraid and the Molkeza did not move a muscle and then. . . .

Quite quietly the Ignet Seed began to shrink again. It began to fold, began to decrease and deflate and sink back into its usual size and then deflate again and Alex remembered when he had held it in his hand. And then it floated by itself and humbly—into the Molkeza's net.

There was a great sigh of Maborian breath. A deep voice came from the back of the crowd.

"Well done, Harri," the Molk declared.

Now the Kylins were parked, two by two, green fur, red fur, black fur and brown, along the Broad Walk that lay to the left of the Pond. They were slung with panniers blossoming to the brim, high with packs like camels, bearing cages with dark wild plants inside, cages with old imprisoned time and cages with the captured song of birds. Each Kylin had a Maborian attendant, each Maborian was booted to the knee and himself had a big pack upon his shoulder and a wine-flask at his belt.

"Now has the wheel turned a little further," murmured Kovor to himself, gazing round rather wistfully as he waited with Charko. "Each moment has no sooner arrived than it flies. Nothing keeps still, yet nothing is lost. We shall be back—yet

already, look, we have left. Hello and goodbye and here we are again."

Uta's voice rang out across the company:

"FIFTEEN MINUTES PLEASE."

Once more the cages hanging low against Buffon's flank were carefully secured and Piperada was satisfied: the Molk's collection was ready to leave. A

quiet smile of relief crossed Corbrey's face, as the last silver trowel was tucked into one of Minsta's great baskets. Dagleff—well, Dagleff wore his master's luggage like some fantastic disguise. *He* was totally obscured by bright shining cauldrons and big full-bellied cooking pots, all stuffed with tattered books and scrolls and battered ladles, and everything clanking madly as he walked. Alex was impressed that even this massive load disturbed the sturdy Kylin not at all.

"TEN MINUTES PLEASE."

"All right, all right, I'm almost ready," the Molk said, "but I'm not quite ready." He turned to Brid and Alex. "If," he began slowly, "if and as and when we reach the other side, when we reach Maboria; and before, and first, that is previous to untying me, or what is left of me . . ." he pushed a parcel each into their hands. "These are yours—I want you to put these on for me."

They were purses, strangely transparent purses and they were filled with feathers.

The twins could hardly speak.

"You have more than earned them here," he said. "They are my thanks, and I would see you wearing them—when I see my Maboria."

"EIGHT MINUTES PLEASE."

At the head of the column the Molkeza waited astride Umbrij, the Seed still seated in her net. She looked set and stern and serious, as if much was still to come. And now Brid was tying a third knot in the silken cloth that masked not only the Molk's eyes, but also his ears and nose. And the Molk sat silently on Bastif while Alex covered the large hands with unfingered gloves and bound his arms firmly against his sides with a wide sash of scarlet. Now the Molk could neither see, nor smell, nor hear, nor touch, the flower of Olbaboth.

"SIX MINUTES PLEASE."

Everything was prepared and in this brief moment of calm the twins thought of themselves. Suddenly the idea of their journey, the very hugeness of the prospect, was overwhelming. Quite deliberately they were abandoning their own country, family and Time.

"But we shan't lose any of our Time," Alex murmured, as much really to reassure himself as to remind Brid.

"No," she agreed. "Kovor said we would return at exactly the same moment. I suppose that very bird will be banging that same snail against that same stone—only the Maborians won't be here."

"FOUR MINUTES PLEASE."

The great black Kylin, carrying Alex, the Molk and Brid, strode easily forward to the head of the procession and stopped beside Umbrij. He was followed by Afghar carrying Thobrusk and the most precious of the wine-skins. Already waiting there was Dagleff, the Ludaz perched triumphantly among his pots. And then came Uta on Hubble and Piperada on Buffon, then Corbrey on Minsta and Kovor on Charko and then the endless column of All Maboria in Exile behind.

The exile was almost over. Slowly and splendidly the laden Kylins proceeded to the Pond, where waiting to receive them, like a great luminous doorway, was the flower of Olbaboth.

The golden light shone dazzling out of the huge, bright, wide-mouthed trumpet flower, and Maborians and Kylins gazed, gazed down into the emerald throat of NOW.

And then Harragong lifted high her net and the Ignet Seed rose by itself, rose and swelled and floated, forward and slowly, just above their heads to lead them down and down the endless gleaming corridor. They advanced—and with a loud yelp of expectant excitement, Umbrij leapt first into the Olbaboth.

. . . And at this moment Alex and Brid heard a new note, a note that came softly otherward, upward, towards them, a brave note that thrust near to them and was followed by others.

There was a voice.

A voice sang of a tree on a green mountain that could remember old age and looked forward, how long it looked forward, to the time when it was young.

"Flothba," Kovor cried. "Flothba still sings across Maboria."

"I vunder if it vill be breakfast time ven ve arrive?" the Ludaz asked thoughtfully behind them. But the twins hardly heard him. Their Molk was silent and he was in their care. Now they were leaving Kew, they were leaving all Kew Gardens, but ahead it was wonderfully green.

If you have enjoyed this book you may also like these

TO VANISHING POINT *by Doreen Norman* 20p
552 52003 9 Carousel Fiction

There was a strange glow in the playground. Leaves were blowing round on the ground, but in a perfect circle. Then Hazel noticed something else, something which, somehow, no-one but herself could see. A girl was standing looking at her, a silver girl, from another planet.

DANNY DUNN TIME TRAVELLER
by Jay Williams and Raymond Abrashkin 25p
552 52005 5 Carousel Fiction

Inventions and experiments always fascinated Danny Dunn, but somehow anything of a scientific nature had a habit of going wrong as soon as Danny managed to get himself involved. Professor Bullfinch had a new machine, a machine to challenge the boundaries of TIME itself. Danny was determined not to be left out, unfortunately for the Professor.

JASON *by Joyce Stranger* 20p
552 52004 7 Carousel Fiction

The pup wasn't wanted, born of a golden Labrador bitch and a giant mastiff. Then Duncan found him, a lonely young boy who needed a friend just as much as Jason needed a loving owner. The closeness between them was only strengthened when Duncan was sent away to school, and then his father had an accident. Jason had to do something.

THE BLACK PEARL *by Scott O'Dell* 20p

552 52008 X Carousel Fiction

The Black Pearl belonged to the old men, with legends and stories to tell to pass the time – or so Ramon Salazar had thought, until he came face to face with the devilfish and the struggle for the pearl began. But Ramon had more than the dangers of the sea to conquer. Others wanted the Great Pearl of Heaven, including the evil Pearler from Seville.

THE PET SHOP *by Martha Robinson* 20p

552 52002 0 Carousel Fiction

The monkey was familiar all right; it was Tony; but what was he doing in the garden? He was supposed to be locked away safely in a new cage at the pet shop Mr. Petravic had just opened next door. Cliff and Miranda decided to try to catch him, but Tony was too clever for them. He had escaped once, and he wanted to stay free.

THE STORY OF MAUDE REED *by Norah Lofts* 25p

552 52010 1 Carousel Fiction

Her grandfather was only a wool merchant and his house was not considered suitable for a young girl of noble blood. Maude was now old enough to be taught the accomplishments of a lady; sewing, music and the art of graceful behaviour. But this was the fifteenth century and her school was to be an old, dark castle.

LOOKING AND FINDING *by Geoffrey Grigson* 25p

552 54007 2 Carousel Non-Fiction

You can find sunken treasure hidden away in some long-forgotten shipwreck, or discover the past through scattered fossils and ancient inscriptions. It depends what you are looking for, how you go about finding it. It depends where you are looking, how you go about getting there. But once the search begins there's no knowing what you might stumble across.

THE WHITE BADGER *by Gordon Burness* 25p

552 54008 0 Carousel Non-Fiction

A badger was born just outside London, in fact only eighteen miles from the city centre. He was discovered by eleven year old Gary and his older brother Phil, who had arrived one day at the author's doorstep with a request to be taken badger hunting. Their first find was unusual, for it wasn't an ordinary badger, it was an all-white, an albino badger. Gary called him Snowball, and this is his story.

TRUE MYSTERIES *by Bob Hoare* 25p

552 54009 9 Carousel Non-Fiction

Tales of the unknown, stories of people who suddenly appear and disappear without explanation, and strange events which present no logical answer, sometimes turning legend into fact, or fact into legend. And always leaving a question mark.